LOVE-HUNGRY PRIEST

A break down is a breakthrough

Sid Custodio
with Cliff Dudley

New Leaf Press

P.O. BOX 1045, HARRISON, ARK. 72601

First Printing, March, 1983

Typesetting by Type-O-Graphics
Springfield, MO 65806 (417-864-4854)

Library of Congress Catalog Number: 82-061308
International Standard Book Number: 0-89221-099-0

DEDICATION

To:
- My God-given, precious Audrey who day by day fills and encourages me.
- My family and friends who also loved and touched me along the way.
- All who desire a more love-filled life.

CONTENTS

PUBLISHER'S PREFACE

Man for centuries has constantly continued his struggle and search for a relationship with God. Sid Custodio is no exception, except he started closer at the Source than most.

Although he was raised and educated in a religious Catholic environment, and even became a priest, Sid was not able to recognize the redemptive power of God through the death and resurrection of His Son, Jesus Christ.

Sid's search continued for a long twenty-five years as a parish priest. Heartache, rejection, alcoholism, and loneliness eventually lead to total collapse, physically and mentally. People began to touch his life and tell him the answer was Jesus and His Holy Spirit.

In this book, LOVE-HUNGRY PRIEST, Sid reveals ALL. In this, his personal story and deliverance, he considers it an honor to commend this book to you, the reader.

—Clifford Dudley
Writer and Publisher

At the author's discretion some of the names have been changed.

1

Filipino Roots

Most of my life I had been secretly ashamed of my family roots. My father, James Custodio, was born in the Philippine Islands and was of Spanish and Filipino parents. He held the position of treasurer of Placer (a town) on the Island of Mindanao. He was educated in Manila.

Many of the Filipinos broke away from the Roman Catholic Church because Rome would not make any of the native Filipinos a bishop. At that time they always had to have a European bishop who had been trained in Rome to be the head of the Filipino church in the area where my father lived. Because of this they rebelled and created a schism—an authority break with Rome. In his early 20's Dad was trained and became a priest in that new breakaway church.

Until Dad was 92 years of age we never knew the reason, but suddenly one day he decided to leave his native land and seek his fortune in Hawaii, picking pineapples for pennies a day. It always seemed strange why a person trained to be a teacher would get on a boat and go to Hawaii to pick pineapples. On his Sixtieth Wedding Anniversary, Dad told us that he left the Philippine Islands because of a break up of a serious relationship with his girl friend.

After two weeks in Hawaii, he came Stateside to San Francisco. There were no jobs for the Filipinos, so he went to Alaska to work a while in the salmon fisheries. He had a tremendous gift of music and always had an old Hawaiian ukulele banjo with him. He never put himself down when people called him "monkey." Dad sang until the afternoon of his death at 94. He took the hurts in and out in a hurry. His music was the way that I'm certain he got rid of the agony.

Dad had a very hard time getting settled, but soon he took a job as a gardener for one of the affluent families of the San Francisco Bay Area.

In the meantime most of my mother's brothers and sisters moved to San Francisco from Ireland. One of her brothers was talking to another Irish man who was eager to marry a pretty lassie from Ireland. So her brother said, "Pay my sister Margaret's fare here and I'm certain she will be glad to marry you."

My mother, Margaret, leaves the family farm outside of the Galway Area back in Ireland to go to San Francisco. Her Irish husband-to-be gets angry when she even says "Hello" to another man. As a result she calls off the wedding and gets a job to pay him for her freight so she can get herself free. Wait until you see how free!

As fate would have it, she goes to work for

the same family where my father was working. Dad is the gardener. Mom is the housekeeper. He's Filipino. She's Irish. This is 1916, so Margaret is twenty-eight.

My mother was aggressive and dominating to the extent that one day when they were paid she said, "Jimmy, why don't we put our paychecks together." He accepts that as a proposal of marriage, and they marry May 27, 1916. The family disowned her for marrying a Filipino, and I would be twenty-one before I would ever meet one of my Irish relatives.

In the State of California at the time, a racially-mixed marriage was illegal. It was absolutely against the law for my mother to marry Jim, my dad. Thank God for a Catholic priest of Our Lady of Guadalupe in San Francisco who married them. From their union were born four children—Margaret, Ed, Jim and me, Sid.

My early childhood was lonely and somewhat sad. I hardly knew my brothers and sister. As a matter of fact, I was in my forties before I had a personal relationship with them. All I know about myself in my early years of life is rather vague.

The family always seemed to hide the fact we were half Filipino. Dad never went any place with us in public. Mom was the dominant force in my life. I was sent to kindergarten at a public school, but from first grade on I was educated in Catholic schools.

I was born on October 4, the day of the Feast of St. Francis. My father said to Mother, "Let's call him Francis."

"No, someone down the street just had a baby and they named him Francis. We can't look like we're copying what they are doing."

"Then name him after my father, Ysidro."

"No, we can't do that. We're in America. We'll make it American and call him Sidney."

Lunch was late at the hospital the day I was born, and when the nun came in with the tray she said to my mother, "I'm sorry lunch is late, Mrs. Custodio, but the cook quit."

"That's all right. My husband can cook—hire him."

Mom was a work-a-holic, taking care of our house and cleaning the homes of the neighbors for pay—always saving the family money. Dad worked at the hospital for twelve years, until a nun came that for some reason didn't like the two Filipino cooks and fired both of them. Then the Second World War came along and Dad was hired to work in the shipyard. What a boon for the racial minorities—some had good-paying jobs at last.

During my grade school years I developed no close friends. There were a few kids on our block that I played with, but basically I was a loner. I was always hurting or empty inside and never could understand why. Perhaps it was the undercurrent of being a mixed breed.

We lived on a two-block street that was more like an alley. Most of my time was spent playing there with the neighbor kids. The first effects of being Filipino came when one of the kids called me a "goo goo," a slang expression some used to call a Filipino. It cut deep into every fiber of my being. How I wanted to run to my parents for comfort and reassurance, but I remained silent and buried the hurt. I blotted out almost everything from those early years. I cannot remember any happy days or any bad days, any birthdays, any Thanksgivings, any Christmases, or anything special about church.

Sports became my way of life when I turned twelve. I was engulfed by playing in a game—any game. That gave me no time to think or be hurt or be empty. A few of us formed a neighborhood club: "The Striking Club," named after my initials. Why? I don't remember, but there is one day I remember most vividly for it was to haunt me for years to come.

I was in the eighth grade, and we were having a meeting of our club in our basement. There was a kid from about a block away that was new in the neighborhood. The basement was dark with little windows up high towards the ceiling. All of a sudden he said, "Let me show you something," and he masturbated!

At first I sat there shocked. Then most of us did it, or at least tried. Little did I know that moment would plague my conscience for years to come and almost drive me to insanity. From that moment I seemed to be posessed with self-centered desires.

I made my spending money by helping my brothers sell newspapers on various corners around the neighborhood. I made a game out of it, trying to get the passing cars to stop and buy from me. I really turned on the charm, and soon had somewhat of a following.

I was now thirteen and loving to meet

people—all people—especially pretty ones. I began to realize that I could affect people with my charm. One day while selling the papers a couple of Italian guys, Joseph and Carlo, said, "Hey, Sid, you want a job?"

"Yes."

"You come, Sid, you come with us."

The job was working in their grocery store. I worked hard six days a week, ten hours a day. All I got was $12 that first week. I knew I had been had, and I ran home to the one that could take care of it all—Mom.

She went to the store and let them have a deserved burst of her anger. They promised to pay me more. That job was crucial. Here I am only thirteen and being launched out into meeting a lot of people. I began loving to meet more and more people. Eventually, they let me wait on people. However, I never revealed who I really was.

There was a beautiful single gal that shopped at the store. I always did love women, and I liked especially to wait on her. Once she said to me, "Sid, I'd like to take you home for dinner some day." When she said that I thought I was an Olympic athlete who had won a gold medal. Every time from that day on when I saw her I would hope she would ask me home, but she never did—to my total disappointment.

Every Sunday I would go to Mass with the family, with the exception of my father. He went to a church in another parish. I often wondered why, but never really cared enough to ask.

My first communion—a major event in a young Catholic's life—is only a blank space to me. Presumably, I was in the second grade and age seven. While in the eighth grade, my preparation for the reception of Sacrament of Confirmation was making me more aware of my sexual problems, but I never dreamed of sharing the real me with anyone. I lived in constant fear because I was lying in the confessional by not telling all my serious sins. Somehow I managed to erase from time to time the nagging guilt. Often I would sit in church and look at the various statues and feel the weight of hell on my conscience. I would pray, "Does anyone else have my problems, God?" I would continue to do penance that I had imposed upon myself. I also lived in fear that the priest would discover my problem.

I really liked the girls but never got close to any of them. I surely thought a lot about them, especially about kissing them—Dorothy—Suzanne—Elizabeth in particular. I put all of my energies into sports, and that gave me a degree of popularity at school—especially with the girls. As a result, in the eighth grade, I was one of the big athletes around campus. I ran for class president. My opponent was a guy named Jack Driscoll, who was very popular, chubby, well-liked and successful. His comment was, "Sid won because all the girls voted for him." I really enjoyed that victory.

My little nephew, Joe, is now in the first

grade. His teacher was a nun, Sister Joan, who looked very Irish to me. She was in her late twenties. Because I had to take care of Joe, I got to know Sister Joan very well. We would spend hours together as she was really big in sports. I was willing to leave sport activities even in order to visit in her classroom, or go to the convent parlor, just to be with her. She would listen to whatever I said. This was the first time I ever shared my personal thoughts and feelings with anyone. I don't remember her saying much. She was the only one to whom I almost revealed the fact that I masturbated.

I'm still going to confession once a month (the students in Catholic schools at that time went once a month). I had never confessed my problem to the priest, which now is the beginning of that serious inner anxiety: "to lie in confession is a mortal sin, plus." They call it a big name, sacrilege, because you've defiled something very holy. I almost confessed my sin to Sister Joan—we had that much of a relationship. A human was actually listening to me.

She would hug me like you hug a child, and to me that felt fantastic. When she hugged me with all her black garb surrounding me, she would say, "You're okay, Sid. You're clean." This was the first time in my life that I was sharing some of my inner feelings and she was giving me back a very important thing. "You're okay. You're special. You're clean." Inside my soul I'm still not making a good confession, and therefore I'm going to hell. I certainly knew what hell was. My knowledge and fear of it far exceeded my thoughts of heaven.

I'm supposed to go to Sacred Heart High School like my two brothers. Because I was an "A" student I was selected to go to St. Ignatius. In those days, it was the one to go to, so to speak, because of the reputation for its standard of excellence.

In my early parochial life, prayers, confession, and religion classes were the way of life, but they never meant much to me or were they life-changing. From time to time we would have special priests come to the school and invite us to consider becoming priests. I would always indicate that I had that desire. The desire for priesthood was inside me early in life. I recall while in grade school building a little altar in my bedroom and "saying Mass."

Sister Joan was really a help to me. *I don't know how I would have made it without her!* She always seemed to say just the words I needed to hear to encourage me. For example, like the time I was sitting in the convent parlor. "Sid," she asked, "have you ever seriously thought of becoming a priest?"

"Sometimes, Sister. Do you think I should?"

"Only you can answer that question, Sid. I would like you to have a special meeting with Father Mahoney. I believe he would be of great assistance to you. Will you meet with him?"

"Sure. I would be glad to," I replied.

Within the next couple of days we had our meeting, and after talking a while Father

Mahoney asked, "Sid, do you want to go to the seminary and study to become a priest?"

I paused for scarcely a moment and quickly replied, "Yes, Father, I believe I would like that."

"Go home and tell your mother."

Everything seemed so matter-of-fact to me. There were no sirens ringing, no skyrockets exploding, I simply said, "Yes." I was in the ninth grade so I didn't think as yet about all the real demands of the priesthood.

My father was never mentioned in public and was somewhat ignored at home. That's why the priest said, "Go tell your mother." He most likely thought my father was dead. The family was never together in public.

I went home, put down my books and yelled, "Mom, guess what? Today I decided that I'm going to be a priest, and next year I'll be going to St. Joseph's Junior Seminary."

Mother looked pleased and simply said, "Sid, that will be fine!"

The entire conversation was all matter-of-fact—nothing exciting at all.

A priest at St. Ignatius selected me to be one of the soda jerks at the school for the following school year. I thought that was wonderful, but because I was going to the seminary I couldn't do it. That same priest, Father "Tiger" McNally (we called him "Tiger" because he paced the floor constantly when he gave us examinations) wrote me a letter during my first month at St. Joseph's:

Dear Sid,
I will always remember your piercing
black eyes as you sat in the first row
of the class. I am so happy that you
have chosen the priesthood as your
vocation.

Father Alfred McNally

Before entering the seminary I had only two buddies that I was even remotely close to. One was John Sinclair, a newcomer to school from Omaha, Nebraska. John liked sports, and so we did everything together. The other was Ernie Rice from the block. John didn't know anything about my "problem" so we weren't that close. Ernie either, although he was in the basement where it all began, but we never talked about it.

2

"Obedience to the Rule"

Seminary begins a new way of life. I now leave home because seminary is also a boarding school. It was rather an awesome feeling to say "good-bye," realizing it would take eleven years before I would become a priest.

I was anticipating making some very close friends, but it wasn't long after I arrived that I began to realize that would never happen. I had become very dependent on Mother, and being away from her was more difficult than I imagined.

My first mail call was a letter from Mom. Every word seemed to unleash emotions within me I hardly realized were there. I ran off to an isolated spot to read it again. I sat there and cried and cried, *How am I ever going to be able to stay here feeling the way I do?* I missed my mother. I was going through a bad case of homesickness. I'm thinking: *I won't make it, I can't go through eleven years of this!*

Mom always took me to movies every week. The theater gave away free dishes, and if you'd bring somebody else you'd get two dishes with an adult ticket. It was always just Mom and me—never Dad. Even on New Year's Eve we would go to a movie to sing in the New Year with the song words on the screen, and the theater organ playing. My mother and father lived in two different worlds. I never remember them even hugging or kissing or showing any kind of affection—never! They didn't even go to the same church. They did nothing together.

At times, if I was bad or something (you had to be almost perfect), Mother had two expressions: "You're good for two things: you are good for nothing, and no good." I don't know how much kidding was in her remarks, but I also knew that she was serious.

When I was bad she'd say, "I'm going to shut my eyes and die." Then she would shut her eyes.

"No, wake up, Mamma, wake up. Come out of it!" It was torment to me.

I'm sitting in that isolated wooded area trying to figure out why I was crying when I got that letter because there was no real relationship with her. She was simply all I had.

All of the "newcomers" were given several hours of orientation. There was one phrase that would guide me for my next eleven years, and that was: "OBEDIENCE TO THE RULE." It was to be absolute or you would be expelled.

Seminary life was all activity based on obedience and discipline—from wake up call at 5:55 A.M. until lights out at 9:30 P.M.

"An active boy," said Father, "will not get into trouble." He continued, "There is one thing we will not tolerate and that is going into another student's room. Never, do you understand that? Never!" None of us could understand that. That should be a time of conversation and making new friendships.

After that session I began to wonder what I had gotten into. However, the system of daily routine soon took over most of my feelings. From 5:55-6:30 A.M.—up, twenty minutes to clean up, down to chapel for a fifteen-minute meditation. In the minor seminary a priest read a meditation to you. I don't remember anything about the meditations. Whether I was too sleepy or didn't want to hear too much of the "spiritual" stuff, I don't know. Remember, all through this I'm carrying unconfessed mortal sins from the past, even though I was no longer masturbating. I had accumulated about eight to nine hundred masturbation mortal sins. I was still going to confession and not confessing those mortal sins. I was conscious of that in the back of my mind so I consciously wouldn't listen to any meditation. I was afraid. I didn't want anything to trigger my subconscious and bring my sins to the conscious where they would bother me or where I would have to confess them. I knew all the time I wasn't going to confess it. I wanted to, but I also didn't want it to bother me.

After meditation there was Mass. I went to Communion every single day for eleven years—except maybe a couple of times when I was sick. As it turned out, it would be Mass and Communion every day *for seven years* in the seminary with all of this internal heavy luggage of mortal sins. God to me was just a scorekeeper, a judge, keeping the official count and waiting to burn me.

My mind was greatly burdened. I didn't

want anything to bother it. I just wanted to be happy and to have fun. Everything is on the external. Everything is superficial other than Sister Joan, and now also Sister Celeste—and probably Jim Morrissey. They weren't deep-sharing friendships, but they were real.

Mass was from 6:30 to 7; breakfast until 7:30; 7:30—clean room every day; 7:55—leave room and do not return until 9:15 P.M. Study was at 8 o'clock in the morning. It was a beautiful system. I had gotten all "A's" at St. Ignatius, first honors every month. At St. Joseph's Seminary there was a half-hour study before every hour class—a tremendous study system. Almost everything was regular high school studies. It was just like an outside Catholic school as there would be one period of religion. There were two classes in the afternoon. Then, of course, there were sports. That was the big thing for me.

Naturally, everything of Sid went into sports. I had to be busy and not think of sin. I was in sports all year: softball, soccer, basketball, track, baseball. I was the all-star in everything except swimming. I couldn't swim. Sports were the big thing in the afternoon. Then it was dinner, walking time, an hour and a half study, night prayers together, then lights out at 9:30. We were never in our room except when making the bed in the morning, and at night when we went to bed.

Of course, you could never step into another person's room. This was just automatic. They saw it as an act of homosexuality—going into another kid's room.

That was it! Even to borrow his pencil was expulsion. There was never a reason to be in another person's room. EXPELLED—we were very conscious of that. As a result, you basically never thought of doing such a thing.

In my class of fifty fellows, there was a very daring maverick: Tommy McMullen— affectionately called "Terrible Tommy" because of his daring escapades. One semester in my third year in the seminary, Tommy challenged us to sleep in each other's room. Automatic expulsion, of course. I don't know if anyone did it, but I know this for a fact: one night around ten o'clock, a classmate, Fred Matlock, sneaked into my room. I'm frozen with fear, to be sure. Then he proceeds to get into my bed. By now I'm petrified and half out of the bed. Fred laughs his fun-devilish laugh. "Exciting, huh, Sid?"

We talk quietly a few minutes and he goes off to sleep. I acted quiet as if I were asleep. When the bell rang at 5:55 A.M., I was so happy to have Fred leap out of bed and rush to his own room. I was a wreck. I hadn't slept a minute all night. That was the most dangerous action in my eleven years of seminary life.

The strict discipline was taking effect. You were allowed to talk in the study hall a few minutes before the bell rang or during sports. If you didn't play sports you'd sit on the bench or in study hall. There was no way to develop a real relationship.

In the seminary rule there was an expression, *"Cave Inimicissimas Amicitias."* It was in Latin and meant: *beware of unfriendly friendships,* but what it said, unfortunately, was, "don't make friendships." I don't know of anyone that developed a deep, intimate friendship. No one had a roommate. You were always alone in individual rooms. There was a bed, a sink, a chest of drawers. You studied in the study hall in minor seminary, never in your room. In the major seminary it was the same thing, except you had a desk and you studied there.

Lights had to be out very shortly after you got to your room.

You couldn't even bring a book to your room to read. Some daring spirits brought books to their rooms and read them under the covers or in the closet, reading by flashlight.

I got tired enough from the daily intensive sports activities that I could sleep.

We had to go to confession every week. You went to the priest's room. He sat in his chair, and there was a kneeler placed next to him. I never got that mortal sin out of my system in my five years of minor seminary. My typical confession was: "Bless me, Father, for I have sinned. It's one week since my last confession. I swore. I told a couple of lies. For these, and all the other sins in my past life, I ask forgiveness." Somehow I could go in there and do that week after week and I did not feel like a phony or hypocrite.

Once a year they would bring priests from outside parishes in for what was called "a general confessional." The psychology behind this was: "Okay, it's nobody you know, it's a stranger. You can get it all out, all your hidden sins, at least once a year and you can make it."

Mom came every visiting Sunday, which was the third Sunday in the month. Dad never came. We went home on Thanksgiving Day from eight in the morning until eight at night; two weeks during Christmas time. We were allowed to go home, even get a job, three months every summer. I always worked to help with expenses at home and to enjoy myself with special treats.

My opinion as to why Dad didn't ever come in the eleven years of my seminary training was that Mom didn't want anyone to know that I had a Filipino dad—so that I wouldn't go through unneeded hassle, in her perspective. I went along with her and never mentioned Dad.

The minor seminary training consisted of six years. There were four years of high school and two years of college. I entered St. Joseph's in the second year of high school, so at the end of my five years of minor seminary I had not masturbated at all. In fact, for the entire eleven years of my priesthood training I did not commit "my hidden sin." In the sense of "I'm going to be a priest, a man of God," I quit. I really bought the idea and dream that I was on my way to being a priest. That's a different ball game. When I went to the seminary I knew that I could not be dirty and be a priest, so I simply quit and shoved it and my fantasizing, for the most part, aside.

I had Sister Joan at least to talk to and hug when I went home on vacation. We still had that special relationship of sharing.

3

St. Joseph's Minor Seminary

Jim Morrissey, a new friend at school is "big" all the way through. He's a friend mainly to talk about sports. There is no intimate communication as we know in deep friendship. I took the responsibility for our relationship being only the "do-it-together-thing." I kept myself locked up at the deeper level. I didn't want to slip and open up too much and bring my shame out in the open. Only Sister Joan is the outlet of deepest listening and talking.

Suddenly, during my second year in the seminary, Sister Joan is sent to another school. I didn't know where, but she left and another nun took her place. Sister Celeste is also very attractive. This is all in my head. Everything but her face is covered. However, I really fell for her, and rapidly she became a friend of mine in the sense of really talking and listening to me like Sister Joan. This woman, however, never hugged me. She thought that was wrong, but she would hold my hand.

I would go wherever she was during the school year or her summer residence, and we would talk for two or three hours, whatever, and hold hands most of the time. That was her rule. I remember wanting to hug, but she'd say, "We can't do that." She was to be my link to sanity from age sixteen until I was twenty-five.

At the seminary sports were far more important to me than religion or sin. Baseball was my favorite sport. Soon the day would come when I would be chosen or drafted into one of the teams. The minor seminary teams were "The Bears," "The Trojans," and "The Ramblers."

Joey, a boy I knew from Catholic grammar school, met me in the hall and said, "Sid, I'm sure glad you enjoyed my letters to you and decided to come to the seminary also. I've been here a year and it's a real blast. By the way, I know how good you are in sports, especially baseball, so when you're up at the plate in the exhibition game be sure to strike out. Everyone will think you're no good and then we'll choose you to be on our 'Bears' team."

My friend Jim Morrissey did the same thing, and, of course, Mike chose both of us. Jim and I felt ecstatic—being "Bears" together.

Often during the general confession, I really went through a type of inner hell. One time I remember most vividly. I was kneeling next to the visiting priest. I had chosen one I had never seen. Supposedly you could go to him and confess everything in your life with no fear, but I had fear of my unconfessed sin, and the fear that day with him was really bothering me. Somehow with him I did review my whole life and confessed quite a bit, but certainly not the masturbation part. After I finished he asked, "What was that about purity, young man?"

I really got shook up because I hadn't said anything about purity, or sins of impurity.

Again he asked, "Did you mention something about purity?"

For a scary moment I thought he knew. I thought that God had let him know my sin. I took a deep breath and said, "Father, I said nothing about purity. I'm clean, Father."

"Go in peace then, young man," he said.

Slowly, I got to my feet and then almost ran from the room. I stood outside the door to regain my composure and thought, *How long can I continue not confessing this hidden sin of mine? Surely I will be condemned to hell forever.* The jolting guilt feelings didn't last long and I threw myself more eagerly into sports activities.

The reason I highlight this is because in a sense sports is our whole life. Intense team competition—complete with meriting personal awards and team trophies. There's no heavy theology the first six years, just tremendous regulations for self-discipline. All the fun for me, and many of us, was in the world of sports. In fact, in that day the seminary was 90% or so athletes or "jocks." The ten percent who weren't were really different from our athletic outlook on life. If you weren't a jock something was missing in your life. If you were seen reading a book often you were not "with it," you were really out of it.

Jim Morrissey and I would do things together all during the summer and Christmas
vacations. In a special way that I feel to this
day, I was very close to him and consider him
my best friend. I guess we talked about everything in life except sin.

The years that followed were rather un-
eventful. Mom continued to visit once a month,
and we made mostly small talk—never
anything real serious. That's the way I wanted
it and liked it.

At the end of my high school years I was
told I would have to be more careful of my
employment as I could no longer work where
there were a lot of women. I was disappointed
that I would not be able to work any more in
the grocery store, meeting lots of people,
mostly women. I'd miss that very much
indeed. This was somewhat the beginning of
our specialized priesthood training, as they
began to separate us more and more from
"worldly influences."

When we had free time from the seminary I
would go to the convent and talk to Sister
Celeste. It seems I always had a woman who
would at least hold hands from eighth grade on
through the seminary years. I had to have this,
I think, or I would have gone crazy and broken
down sooner than I did.

I never told my seminary peers where I
was going. Never. My visits would have been
under heavy suspicion. From the large amount
of time I spent there, they would have considered it most unhealthy.

That summer I worked in Yosemite National Park. A little restaurant hired two of us from the seminary. A religious family owned it. They also let the Jesuit priests come on vacation and sleep in the cabins behind the restaurant. Bernie, a boy in the class ahead of me at school, and I hired out as dishwashers. To my great inner joy, the owners had a beautiful red-headed niece named Rose. Naturally, I instantly fell in love with her. It was another of my fantasies.

One particular night they were going to have a weiner roast at the nearby beach at midnight. I had to work until ten, so I got brave and asked, "Rose, can I see you when I get there?"

She answered, "Yes."

I could hardly contain myself until ten o'clock that night. Those dishes were cleaned and stacked in record time so that I would have as much time as possible at the beach party with Rose. When I got to the beach area she had saved a place on the blanket next to her for me. I thought that was super. We ate a couple of hot dogs and joined in on the community sing. It was fun, daring—even a little frightening. I took her home afterwards and kissed her. My entire nervous system vibrated for well over an hour with happy excitement. I could hardly wait to see her again.

For an eighteen-year-old I was rather naive, but yet very forward. I had heard one of the waitresses sing so I told the owner, "She is really great. You should have her sing at the Fire Falls program tonight."

To my surprise he said, "I'll talk to her and give her a chance tonight."

I asked Rose if she would go with me. Again, she answered "Yes."

I made arrangements for Joe, a friend of mine, to work for me.

The walk to the falls was delightful. I finally got up enough nerve to take Rose's hand. So there we are, a priest candidate and a beautiful redhead walking down the road hand in hand, when who drives up but one of the Jesuit priests that's staying in one of the cabins!

I panicked and thought to myself, *I've had it. He'll tell my supervisors.*

"Hi, Sid. Hi, Rose," he called and drove away.

Joe, who was supposed to work for me, didn't show up, so I was fired. My newly-aroused emotions made it very difficult to leave Rose.

Most of the guys from seminary got together and played baseball on Wednesday nights. I'd tell Jim Morrissey that I'm madly in love with Rose. "Jim, I think I'm going to marry her."

Jim turned to me and said, "No, no, Sid. You're a twelve-year-man. You must go all the way."

The seminary never heard a word about my being fired, as the Catholic owners of the resort were in no way connected to the seminary. All the guys got to know about it, and as a result teased me about Rose, Rose. They even put on a play about my love affair. "One Kiss," they called it.

Jim and myself really are into the game of winning. We like sports, but we also like to win. I sensed that something seemed to be bothering Jim, but I really wasn't intimate enough with him to ask what was wrong.

Jim was a handsome Irish guy with a volcanic temper. He was also very tender, yet an effervescent super-salesman. In those early seminary days if I had a friend it was Jim Morrissey. I love him deeply to this day.

I was sitting under a tree when Jim approached me and said, "Sid, I'm going to leave the seminary."

"You're going to what?" I asked in startled unbelief.

"That's right. I'm going to leave. My confessor asked me to stay three more months, and I promised I would. Yet, I am certain I won't change my mind. You know, Sid, I'm the father type. I simply cannot go through life single." His remarks devastated me like a sudden midwest tornado.

Jim stayed the entire semester and waited until we played the big game against "The Ramblers"—our biggest rival. He wanted one last chance to stomp on them. Reality came to grips with me. My only semblance of a friend was leaving and I would have to go on alone. On the day of his departure I asked permission to go with Jim to catch the bus. I carried one of his suitcases and tried to make some small talk.

"Sid, I really appreciate your coming with

me to the bus. Sorry I'm not sticking it out, but it just isn't for me. You'll make it through, you are going all the way. You are a twelve-year-man."

I stood there almost numb as I saw the bus approaching. How I wanted to throw my arms around Jim and tell him I'd miss him more than he would ever know. All I managed to choke out was, "Good luck, Jim." At that he boarded the bus, and I stood there alone. I didn't cry as we walked to the bus but now nothing could hold back the tears.

Over and over I heard Jim's words, "You'll make it. You are a twelve-year-man."

A twelve-year-man. I thought, *What about that? What am I doing here? What is this all about anyway? Will I ever be free of all this inner guilt? Life is almost more than I can take.* I shook myself and said, "Sid, don't talk like that. You have chosen this life and now you must give it all you've got and more. You have chosen the highest calling man can choose to make. Isn't that what the confessor just said? Now believe it—and go to work."

We had the "Big Brother" system at the seminary. We would pick a freshman and write weekly letters to him. For the most part the letters were simply to encourage one another. When we'd come face to face with the person, it would all be very brief and surface conversation as we were only friends on paper. When I was a freshman my big brother was Fred Hanley. He is now an Archbishop on the West Coast. I knew he was my "brother," but all you said was in the notes. You basically didn't see or talk at length to the ones outside your own class. Our youthful letters were serious, but in reality they were really about nothing significant. We never discussed our real intimate problems. Everything, for the most part, was superficial.

For eleven years we attended classes on Monday through Saturday, with every Thursday off. On Thursdays I'd play ball, clean my room in the morning and do laundry. On designated Thursdays we could go for a walk outside the seminary boundaries. We could not go alone, only in groups of six or more. We would go to a store for an ice cream, candy, etc. It was always a popular walk of wonderful freedom.

We were allowed to smoke during the third year of high school. It was a big experience on the first Thursday of our junior year. We all bought a pack of cigarettes and then smoked the whole pack. Crazy, but to most of us it was a big thrill.

On another day at the ice cream store, some guy met us in the store and asked, "What are you guys?"

"Oh, we're seminarians—studying to be priests," was our sheepish reply.

He looked at all six of us and replied, "You mean if there was a good-looking brawd here none of you would go for her?"

We looked at each other, blushing, got up and left the store without answering. Not one of us could be open and direct enough to discuss the loaded question with each other on the way back home.

One other memorable time on one of our *freedom walks*, we passed a Drive-In that sold beer, as well as soft drinks. That particular spot was off limits for us. Some of us dared to break the rule and went in and bought a soft drink.

The dean of discipline was a really sly guy and was parked with another priest across the road and saw us come out with the bottles in hand. He had caught us red-handed. His face reflected his cunning victory. He wrote our names down on paper and we were grounded for several "freedom Thursdays."

That dean of discipline really thought he had the whole world by the tail. He seemed to really get a thrill making us "toe the straight and narrow line"—and believe me, he saw to it that we did everything he told us to do. He wasn't hated or anything like that. He simply was never listed highly on anyone's popularity poll. I must admit he added a dimension of fear to the seminary environment for me.

In my later seminary years, a different relationship would develop between the dean of fear—Father Michael (or "Mick") Killian—and myself. As a college student I would have "Father Mick" as my public-speaking instructor (a tough, yet excellent teacher), and as a friendly, though fierce, Irish "handball" opponent. In the classroom, he was clearly my talented mentor; on the "handball" court it was a grueling toss-up of mutual admiration.

When I graduated from the minor seminary, the dean's personality and mine—each strong, clever, and competitive—were the same, but the element of fear from my perspective had evolved into a genuine, though quiet, respect.

We had very little to say about what happened at the seminary. However, the whole student body was allowed to vote for the president of the Sodality. The Sodality officers consisted of four students who would lead the total assembly of students and faculty in a prayer meeting for fifteen minutes every Sunday.

I was voted president and it was a distinction that made my insides glow—temporarily at least. That was the only vote we had in the whole school. One of my jobs, however, was to lead the singing, and I couldn't sing. I don't know whether they voted me in because I was an athlete or if they really knew that I couldn't sing. So every time I gave the opening note of one particularly difficult Latin hymn (*Salve Regina*) it was so awful they could hardly go on with the whole song. Once the priest moderator became very upset and said, "I guess you are popular with the kids, Sid, but you certainly don't know that note."

Each Sunday they had to drill me in starting the song. Today I can start that song any time, any place, and it always makes me smile—it's that kind of a nostalgic memory.

Other than the one time when I told Jim Morrissey "I'm going to marry Rose," and his reply, I never thought of leaving the seminary again.

I graduated from St. Joseph's Minor Seminary with special honors called "magna cum laude'' (with great distinction). Mom and brother Ed came. However, my father was not there. Strange, but I didn't even miss him. This fact hurts my insides even as I write this about Dad. By now I'm living in another world. When anyone would ask me, "You Italian, Sid?" I either wouldn't answer or say, "Sure I am." I could not bring myself to say, "I'm Filipino and Irish." I was ashamed to admit it.

Seminary baseball champions. Sid (bottom right), age 18.

4

St. Patrick's Major Seminary

My years at St. Patrick's major seminary started in September. This was a brand new system and way of life—as different as sunset and sunrise. It is here you had to come to grips with yourself and become an independent, self-motivating, disciplined person. In the major seminary you finish two more years of college. It's like regular college work and you get your regular B.A. in Philosophy and English.

In these two years you're much freer. All studying is in your room, where there is a large-size wooden desk. This is where I found that I had little or no discipline in studying regularly, or in making beneficial use of the unsupervised time.

There is still that line barrier that nobody can come into your room. Yes, still automatic expulsion for being found in another's room. Every Thursday you can sign up to go out on your bike or take a walk in a group of three or more. The only stipulation is that you must return by 5:30 P.M.

I began to do all my studies at the last minute. I no longer had that high level of accomplishment because I didn't have any study habits. As a result I dropped to a "B" average, or "B+" at the most.

Some of the fervency of the sports system from the minor seminary is downgraded in the major seminary program. Yet there are still class teams and the friendly-and-ferocious competition continues. However, gone are the awards and trophies for individuals and teams. I missed that part a great deal, since much of my self-esteem and athletic daydreaming was based on the athletic blocks that I won, the track records I set, and the adulation of the younger kids in the seminary. All these achievements, along with the scholastic honors, somehow enabled me to block out of consciousness—almost totally—the awareness of my secret, past sins of impurity—sins that I felt made me a terrible sinner. I always held on to the slim hope that someday I would be delivered from such a fear-filled, guilt-filled internal prison.

After two years of major seminary life in Menlo Park, California, I began experiencing a serious amount of inner tension—complete with clamminess of skin and irregular palpitations in the chest area. A major crisis was facing me and my hidden sins—because I was nominated by the priest faculty to receive the Clerical Tonsure, the beginning ceremony of seven steps that culminate four years later in the conferral of the Sacrament of Holy Priesthood.

However, months before the time of Tonsure, that ceremony where we got our heads shaved and received our clergy robes, fear and nightmares were overtaking me. My mind was showing telltale marks of an impending nervous breakdown. How could I ever take the vows to become a cleric when all my sins of the past nine years had accumulated on my soul? I had successfully buried the warning of the catechism: "WHAT IS MEANT BY A 'BAD CONFESSION'?" A "bad confession" is one in which the penitent deliberately conceals a mortal sin. This renders the confession invalid and sacrilegious, and all future confessions invalid and sacrilegious until the sin is confessed.

During a special series of talks to prepare us for the ceremony I was told to examine my entire life—and I did. Then I realized that I had to deal with the "bad confession." I fully remembered the instruction: **"WHAT MUST A PERSON DO WHO HAS KNOWINGLY CONCEALED A MORTAL SIN IN CONFESSION? A person who has knowingly concealed a mortal sin in confession must confess that he has made a bad confession, tell the sin he has concealed, mention the sacraments he has received since that time, and confess all the other mortal sins he has committed since his last good confession."**

I was especially worried about my unworthy reception of the Sacrament of Confirmation during my eighth-grade year in Catholic grammar school. With mortal sins on my soul, I had dared to receive that sacrament which makes us soldiers and witnesses of Jesus Christ under the powerful gifts and guidance of the Holy Spirit. I felt so terrible and dirty about what I had done to something so holy and sacred.

Confirmation, one of the most serious and awesome experiences in the church, I had defiled. To the worthy and informed Catholic, Confirmation should be an experience essentially comparable to the Pentecost event in the lives of the first believers in Jesus Christ. The sacred Scriptures describe that power-filled phenomenon in Acts 2:1-11. This totally changed the timid believers into courageous public witnesses of God's great works of love.

I had concealed my mortal sins of impurity from the priest in the confessional a number of times. In burying my sins and in attempting to keep the heavy guilt from bothering me, I closed my mind and heart to the powerful reality of the Sacrament of Confirmation. Even though I was thirteen years old at Confirmation time, I do not remember anything about that once-in-a-lifetime sacrament ceremony ... not even the name of the Bishop who conferred the Pentecost Sacrament upon us.

Suddenly, I felt I was certainly doubly damned. I started worrying whether I was confirmed or not because I took Confirmation in mortal sin. Now my mind is spinning, not only that I haven't confessed that sacrilegious sin, but maybe not even confirmed now, and that would mean that I could not take this Tonsure step tonight. I didn't want to make another "bad confession."

The time of Tonsure was eight o'clock. It was six o'clock. I only had two hours to go. I finally got the courage to go to our seventy-year-old priest, Father Pierre Redon. Everyone knew him as a saint, and many priests in the diocese would come in on their days off for counseling and confession. He was like some of those famous saints that you have heard about in the Catholic Church. As I approached Father Redon's room, my feet were as though they were shackled. Each step down the long corridor was full of pain and anguish. I became so weak that I felt that I would never be able to lift my arm to even knock on his door. However, as I did lift my arm to knock on the door, I felt like running and giving up for I was so weak. But as though someone else had lifted my hands, I began to pound on the door, almost screaming, "Father Redon, Father Redon, I need to see you. Please, Father, I need to see you right away."

Slowly the door opened and the saintly priest looked at me with gentle eyes and said, "Sidney, please come in."

"Father," I said in a panting, agonizing voice, "hear my confession. For God's sake hear my confession and help me be free of this terrible guilt that I carry on my heart."

He looked at me, put his purple sacramental vestment on, and said, "Be calm, my young son."

I breathed deeply, and my mind raced, *How will I do it? How will I do it? I have hidden it all these years.* Finally, I calmed down enough to confess to this Christ-like priest. Very slowly I said, "Bless me, Father, for I have sinned. It has been nine years since my last good confession. Father, I have lived in mortal sin these past nine years, for you see, when I was in the eighth grade, I masturbated and never confessed it. I have made literally hundreds of bad confessions, most of them as a seminarian. Can I ever be forgiven for such offenses? Oh, Father, I am sorry, truly sorry for these and all the sins of my past life." Tears by now were running down my cheeks. Still I thought there was no hope, and I felt that my being Tonsured this evening was completely impossible. Father Redon would stop it. Surely, he would stop it and I would be expelled.

Slowly the priest's eyes met mine and he said, "My son, Sidney, we are all weak. Yes, we are indeed weak. Only God is strong, and He lovingly forgives you. You are fine now, Sidney, you are fine. Rejoice in this wonderful step you will take in a few hours. Go now, my son, and for your penance, I want you to say one 'Our Father' to our God who loves us so bountifully."

At that he reached forth his hand and touched my head with tenderness. Then he lifted his hand to make the sign of the cross over me as he said, "Sidney, I absolve you from your sins in the name of the Father and of the Son and of the Holy Spirit. Go now in peace to love and serve our loving God."

Slowly, I reached forth and grasped his hand and said, "Thank you, Father. Thank you, Father. Thank you, Father."

I left the room. Outside I found myself dazed, bewildered and confused. I stood for some time at a window overlooking a courtyard garden. I was dumbfounded as I reflected—my nine years of torture and anguish of hiddenness and heaviness seemed such a waste. *One "Our Father," I thought, one simple "Our Father" penance for nine years of hell. For all of this I only have to say one prayer, and only once! What's wrong with me? Where did I go wrong?*

Something in me at that moment snapped. My mind couldn't handle what had just happened. I thought the truth in confession would make me free and clean, but instead something new was troubling my jumbled mind. Little did I know, but that moment was the beginning of deeper agony and pain than I had ever known. For some strange reason at that moment doubts entered my mind and I was going to be tortured by these harassing doubts for years. The specific theological name for this torturesome, mental aberration is SCRUPULOSITY—a state of constant guilt from real or imaginary sins—mostly the imaginary, unreal ones.

Here I was standing outside the room of a recognized saintly priest. Later I would realize he spoke the forgiving words from God Himself, and I was now caught in the devil's workshop of focusing only on me and my cleanness and my guilt. ME. ME. ME. If only I had turned to this loving God and turned over everything to His care—me and all my disturbing doubts. Instead, I asked myself, *Did I tell him everything? How could I catch up for all those years in just ten minutes? Did I forget to tell Father some important sins? Why is it so simple?*

For the next hour between that confession to Father Redon and the Tonsure Ceremony I wondered now what sins I had committed within the last hour. Even as I was dressing up slowly in my black and white robes I was in agony, pain, unbelief, doubt and confusion. As I walked down the chapel aisle I kept questioning myself, *Am I clean? Am I okay with God?* I didn't celebrate anything that evening. Every moment was agonizing torture.

Sid and Mom on visiting day, Major Seminary, 1949.

5

Scrupulosity

While a scriptural psalm was being sung by the choir, the ceremony of conferring Tonsure took place. Each candidate bowing slightly, knelt before the Bishop while that church leader cut some hair from the candidate's head in five places, so as to form a cross—the church symbol of sacrificial dedication in God's clerical service.

At the same time as the cutting of the hair, the Bishop pronounced the following words, which each candidate repeated after him:

> "The Lord is the portion of my inheritance and my lot. It is you who will restore to me my inheritance" (Psalm 15:5).

Having tonsured all of us, the Bishop rose, turned to us and prayed for us: "Grant, we beseech Thee, Almighty God, that these thy servants may forever persevere in Thy love, for it is because of their love for Thee that we have tonsured them today. May they persevere in Thy love; and do Thou keep them forever without stain through Christ our Lord. Amen."

Yes, during the ceremony I repeated after the Bishop everything he told me to say, and he cut the hair of my head in the form of a cross. I was then a priestly cleric, but I didn't feel like I was anything. I was a bundle of doubts and fears, imprisoned in my own little world, the inside of my head. I had been a *secret sinner* before my confession and Tonsure. After that confession, I had become a *secret scrupulous person* with all the attendant self-inflicted torture of that condition. Though many seminarians congratulated me that night with genuine and back-slapping gladness, I remember that I simply smiled back on the outside, while on the inside I was focused on the attacking doubts. I was more glad that summer vacation started immediately after Tonsure so that I could be by myself. Little did I realize that I had simply traded in one secret mental slavery condition for another.

As soon as summer vacation began I got a job working for a San Francisco construction company. Even as a cleric I was allowed to do this. My first work assignment was as a laborer in the renovation of St. Boniface's School.

Constantly mental doubts accused me of sinning seriously and, therefore, being out of the state of God's grace. I would spend each lunch time going over to St. Boniface's Church, pushing the button that called a particular priest for confession, and confessing my simple real sins and a long list of imaginary sins. I was now living in the constant fear that I had committed a mortal or deadly sin. From my training I knew if I died with one unconfessed serious sin, I would be condemned to hell eternally.

No one knew I was in this mental trouble because I always went to different priests, and remained anonymous to them.

My imaginary sins usually centered on fantasies connected with girls. Even if I imagined kissing one, I had to confess it as a mortal sin. Here is one example of the crazy condition I was now in. I was on the bus one day going home and saw a gal who was topless in a car that drove by my bus. Result? I felt obliged to go to confession at once because I had sinned grievously in sexual thought. This mental condition of scrupulosity was exhausting and I didn't know how to handle it. My mind was so mixed up that almost any thought was a mortal sin.

I never had a God-consciousness or any kind of personal relationship with Him. My life was based simply on church dogma. It was just human teaching for the most part. God, as I perceived Him then, was constantly marking the scoreboard to determine if it was heaven or hell for Sid Custodio. In my confused world of self, hell was easily winning. I was a loser.

The Sixth Commandment, "Thou shalt not commit adultery"—which includes any thought, word or act connected with it was the commandment that was fouling me up.

My ignorant, sick mind latched onto the church teaching about *any thoughts* concerning these sixth and ninth commandments could be mortal sins. With my scrupulous mentality, I felt any sex thought that flashed into my head was a mortal sin—whether I wanted to entertain that thought or not. I was trapped in this imaginary world, one in which I was slowly dying mentally, emotionally and physically.

Here I was a young, athletic, intelligent, socially-oriented person at the effervescent age of twenty-one and I was somehow, without any realization, certainly on the road to self-destruction. I wasn't committing any actions that were serious sins. I wasn't even masturbating. Yet, flashing thoughts or words that I happened to hear were killing me.

After I confessed hundreds of times, I still didn't know a personal God of love and truth who could free me to healthy reality. I wanted to be what I thought was perfect in every way after such a sinful, secret past. I soon became withdrawn, different, and very quiet at times. I'd be with the guys, but as we were talking, I'd be thinking, *Did I have a dirty thought two hours ago?* Suddenly my whole waking life was warring against sin. We would walk after every meal and talk. I would occasionally say "hell," then I would think, *When did I commit the last sin, or did I?*

I still played sports, but before playing, sometimes while playing, I would think, *What did I do last that was a sin?* I was going through a personal hell, but I didn't tell anyone. Later when I told a couple that I was scrupulous and what I went through mentally they said, "You are kidding! This is Sid, the jovial, outgoing person. You're talking to everybody here, everybody on the streets, every waitress. You walk up to everyone. If Kennedy were here you'd say, 'I'm Sid. You are John Kennedy.' Sid, you have got to get over this sick kick.''

Yes, I was changing—for the worse—in becoming more inward and pensive concerning my unreal world. However, I wanted no one to really know what was going on inside me. On the external side of me I determinedly summoned my energies to maintain the happy-go-lucky, likeable appearance that people expected or wanted. This way of living, smiling on the outside and crumbling on the inside, was to be my lot for the last four years in the seminary culminating in priestly ordination.

The four years before priesthood are all theology. This is the systematic study of God, using the philosophical approach to the sources of truth, namely the sacred Scriptures (the written Word of God), and the sacred traditions (spoken Word of God handed down through history).

The two main branches of theological study in which we advanced seminarians were immersed were Dogmatic Theology (the official teachings of the Roman Catholic Church), and Moral Theology (the ethical rules of behavior for all baptized Catholics). What happened to all of us was that we were taught a definite set of beliefs and morals that were gathered and organized by various theology experts with varying philosophies or points of view. I do not recall great emphasis on the prime source of the Word of God. Most assuredly, we did not go to the Holy Scriptures FIRST with open minds and hearts asking the Holy Spirit to guide and enlighten us with the GOOD NEWS and truth that God shares with people to set them free to live victorious, practical lives.

In my daily life today I go primarily to the Sacred Scripture to see what God is telling me for the present challenges and struggles. The Scriptures are love letters to Sid from God Himself. Then in my major seminary years, it was: God is THIS or the church is THAT. Then it was basically some other human being expressing the beliefs and rules as he organized them into some particular system or school of thought. I realize now that the loving, powerful Word of God could have changed my personal journey toward self-destruction. As it was, I started slipping in my studies. My mind couldn't focus on studying because of "When did I last sin" syndrome.

There was no one-to-one relationship with the Lord all through the major seminary, partly because the system said, "Don't get too close in any relationships." During those last four years, while in that unreal world of doubt and darkness, I was suspicious of everyone. I even had a schoolmate who did absolutely nothing wrong, but because he was an intellectual I thought he might be a homosexual. I was so confused that I decided I would go and tell my confessor. I had to stay pure and without sin. I became the "Big Judge."

The RULE said, "Be careful of harmful, unfriendly friendships" (*CAVE AMICITIAS INIMICISSIMAS*), the warning Latin words boldly stated. When I went to the priest and told him what I thought he asked, "Who is it?"

I told him and he said, "No, I think that he's all right. He does like books and everything but, Sid, that doesn't make him any more homosexual or strange than you. Don't say another word about this to anyone. Do you hear me, Sid? To no one!"

Since the priest cleared me of any responsibility, I gladly kept quiet. Thank God he had more sense than I did. Meanwhile, I kept writing long letters to Sister Celeste. During vacations I was going every week or two to see her, just to hold her hand and talk, and talk and talk. I hadn't told this part of my life to any confessor for all those years. I did not think there was sin involved, but I didn't want to know if there was either. I was not bothered internally by this simple, sincere relationship with Sister Celeste. I thank God to this day for those warm, shining moments of sanity and sharing.

The next several years of my priesthood preparation were a maze of study, study, confession, confusion and chaos. Days turned into weeks, weeks into months and months into years. Suddenly it was time to take the final steps toward becoming a Catholic priest. How I made it to this point, I will never understand. Inwardly I was a total mental wreck. All of this was well hidden, of course. No one, not even Mother, could detect that anything was amiss. My external appearance and behavior around people were still basically normal—even outgoing and friendly.

I suppose what remaining mental balance I

enjoyed was the result of my great amount of youthful zest for life and sports, and the lighter, refreshing moments of boarding-school life, seminary style, of course.

Though the lighter moments were mainly on days off and outside the seminary, there were also unique happy times and doings inside the serious and somber classrooms in the seminary building.

As we neared the priestly ordination year our theology naturally took on a more practical side: the pastoral dimension of priestly service. We practiced solemn baptisms on a dime-store baby doll. Her name was Gloria Mundi, Latin for "the glory of the world." Those baptism practices were fun-filled, yet they began to deepen our realization that OUR ordination day was not too far away.

6

Ordination Day

Before the actual day of ordination, there were many papers to sign, making various pledges and promises to the church. This was a tremendous strain on me because I was worried if my ordination to priesthood would be valid, if there were serious sins in my life, if there were conditions that I could not meet. Instead of a time of rejoicing and gladness, it was a time of mountain-size worry and perplexities. My mind was so terribly confused. If I had only known then what was ahead for me as a priest I would have run for my life.

Finally the day of ordination came. It was a great day in my life; all of the solemnity and joy of a marriage feast, with Jesus Christ Himself participating. For some reason all of my problems, frustrations, doubts and worries seemed to vanish for a large portion of that very special day. It was a day of celebration, a day of high excitement, the day that I'd prepared for for eleven long, frustrating years.

Our personal invitations to our ordination had been sent, and our families sat according to the lot that they had drawn. My family, by the luck of the draw, drew the very first pew. I couldn't believe it. This would be the first time my father would be around me in a clerical situation, even though I had been in that environment for eleven years. As only the Spirit of God would have it, he ended up sitting in the first row with Mother for all to see. Every picture taken of the audience would have my Filipino father sitting in the front row next to my Irish mother.

We were called to the front of the sanctuary to stand before the altar. Our names were called out in their Latin form, and we all, one by one, answered in Latin *"ADSUM"*— which means "I am here, I am ready." Then we took one step forward, showing that we were willing to accept this office and dignity of the priesthood, to be another Christ. What an awesome thought.

All of us then lay prostrate, signifying that we were humbly nothing without God, and that we were giving our entire life to the service of God. For a moment as I was there prostrate on the floor I wondered if I had the right intention necessary for a valid ordination: this thought would bother me later in my priestly life.

Bishop Mitty then prayed a silent prayer that we would all be anointed with God's graces sufficient to meet our calling.

We then returned to our positions standing, and were called forth one at a time. Carefully he placed his hands on each of us and prayed quietly, "Almighty Father, creator and possessor of heaven and earth. Most High God, You have sent Your Son, Jesus Christ our Lord and Saviour, as the one High Priest. Pour forth your Holy Spirit and His blessings now upon Sidney Custodio to be your priest forever in the name of the Father, and of the Son, and of the Holy Ghost. Amen."

This was an awesome moment and it was one through which I'm sure God was reaching me. After these quiet moments we returned to our regular places. More prayers of celebration followed. The most important prayer was: "Therefore, we beseech Thee, Almighty Father, invest these thy servants with the dignity of the priesthood. Almighty Father, You have sent Your Son, Jesus Christ our Lord and Saviour, as the one High Priest. Pour forth your Holy Spirit and His power upon these men, anointing them as priests forever according to the order of Melchisedech. Fill them with all the graces needed to be other Christs in their priestly service forever in the name of the Father, Son, and the Holy Ghost." This was the moment of priestly ordination conferred.

In comparison, the Annapolis graduating midshipmen exuberantly would be tossing their caps into the air. Our hearts at their deepest level, now ordained hearts, were performing the clerical equivalent—leaping with pure joy.

But the ordination was not over yet. We were not yet dismissed. The solemn ritual continued. The Archbishop next invested us with the priestly vestments. First, the ordaining church leader put the clerical stole (similar to a long, untied tie) around my neck and said, "Sidney, receive the burden of the

Lord; for His burden is sweet and His cross light." A little later I returned to the Archbishop's chair, knelt at his feet, and received the chasuble vestment, the large outside garment that hangs down the front and back of a priest celebrating the Sacrament of the Mass. "Receive, Sidney, this priestly garb by which Christian love is signified; for God is powerful to increase your love and the perfection of your work."

"Deo Gratias" (Thanks be to God), I answered.

As I write these biographical words to share my love-hungry, early years and ordination ceremony, I am simply and sincerely touched by the quiet realization that much truth is found in the church prayers of ordination. However, the prayers meant little to me in my confused state.

After the priestly vestments were placed upon us, there was a special ceremony involving the anointing of the hands. At that moment Bishop Mitty took oil that had been specially blessed and again called us forth. He poured the sacred oil upon our hands and anointed them. "Vouchsafe, O Lord, to consecrate and sanctify these hands by this our anointing and our blessing, that whatsoever they shall bless may be blessed, and whatsoever they shall consecrate be consecrated and sanctified, in the name of our Lord Jesus Christ."

"Amen," I answered.

He then wrapped my hands in special white cloths—the "bands," we called them.

They had been prepared for each of us. Now our hands were prepared to do priestly service and sacraments. Our hands were now those of Jesus Christ extended. Sister Celeste had made the white hand wrappings for me. This was an honor for both her and me.

I was then called forth again, dressed in the priestly vestments. The Bishop then presented me with a personal silver chalice. It had been made for me by a friend, Patrick McCoy, and I would use it daily at Mass or any occasion when the Eucharist would be celebrated. As the Archbishop and I jointly held the chalice, he prayed and blessed it.

I called my chalice "The Imitation of Christ." The base was formed in a semi-circle as though it were half of a globe. Priests are called for the service of all people. On the very base was a crown of thorns, which was a symbol of life containing struggle and suffering. On the chalice stem was Mother's gold wedding ring that she had given me to be used in the making of the priestly chalice. It would always be a symbol of special joy and commitment between God and me, between Mom and me.

Now we were ready for the final moments of the solemn ceremony. The white outer garment, or chasuble, that had been placed upon us had been tucked in so that it would not drape all the way to the floor. There was special symbolism for that garment being folded until the end of the ordination rites. Now the chasuble vestment, the garment of love, was released, falling to its full length. This symbolized that we were now covered with God's love and that our priestly service to God's people should always be done in love. As the robes were unfolded, the Archbishop prayed over each of us: "Sidney, may the Lord clothe thee with the robe of love and innocence."

The twenty newly-ordained priests of the Archdiocese of San Francisco then stood on the steps of the Cathedral sanctuary for the first time. We were now facing the large congregation of people assembled for our ordination to the Catholic priesthood. All twenty of us in unison made the sign of the cross. As Roman Catholic priests, we said for the first time the following official church blessing: "May the power of Almighty God descend upon you and remain forever. Amen."

It was then that my own mother, father, brother, and Sister Celeste knelt in front of me, and I blessed them as a priest. I dared somehow for the first time to reach out and touch as a priestly instrument of God Himself.

I drove home with Mom, Dad, and my brother Ed. I was still somewhat troubled in my spirit, wondering what was going to happen next in my unfolding personal odyssey.

When I arrived home my father called me into the living room. As I went in, I have to admit I was somewhat shaken and fearful, for in eleven years we had had little or no communication. Suddenly our eyes met, and without hesitation he said, "Father Sid, would you hear my confession?" I thought my heart would leap out of my chest.

What! I thought, *My father wants me, his son, to hear his confession?!* I tried to gain my composure. As I went to the adjoining room to get my priestly vestment, I thought my legs would buckle under me.

I've had no relationship with my father. We'd never been on the same wave length. *Oh, God above, what is he going to say? What is he going to tell me? Is he going to pour out his anguish and hurt because his son and wife have been ashamed of him? Is he going to spill forth the years of anger because I never wanted him to come and see me?* How will I handle this? What will I say? My first confession will be that of my own father.

Slowly I returned to the living room. I had placed the stole over me and sat in a chair. My father knelt beside me and again looked into my eyes. To try to break the intensity of the moment I said, "Sure, Pop, sure it's great to hear your confession." I thought to myself with awe and trepidation, *Wow, what a way to start a priestly life!*

My father then looked at me intently and said in very reverential manner, "Bless me, Father, for I have sinned," and began to mention his sins as any penitent does. In a matter of moments I knew my father like I had never known him. Oh, how simple it was, and he had such tenderness. He was coming to his son, a new Catholic priest, to ask for forgiveness. Emotionally, however all internal, I was hugging, squeezing and kissing my father, throwing my arms around him, having a love affair. I'm celebrating an intimate experience for the first time with my father! There was no bitterness. All the fears that I had internally about my own life and personal guilt were not at my father's confession. It was pure joy, but all I could do was give him a silent hug, a fantasy kind, because there was no real hug. There was no squeeze. I sat there and could not let him verbally know how much I loved him, honored him, and respected him for what he was doing.

When he finished there were tears streaming from his eyes, as there were mine. I placed my hand upon his shoulder. I wanted to cry out, "Dad, Pop, I love you," instead I regained my composure and pronounced the absolution: "In the name of Jesus Christ I forgive you your sins. For your penance I give you five 'Our Father's' and five 'Hail Mary's.'"

Oh, if that were today, his penance would be: "Dad, to celebrate God's great love for us and our special love for each other, let's sing together a stanza of 'Amazing Grace.'"

As he rose to his feet, he took my hand and simply said, "Thank you, Father Sid." In his voice and in mine, love was there, but it was all unspoken. To my knowledge Mother never knew about this special event in my father's and my life. Of course, as a priest those moments were sacred and secret and nothing could be shared.

7

St. Raphael

Sunday, two days after my ordination, I would celebrate the solemn high Mass in my own parish church of The Sacred Heart of Jesus. However, before that, on Saturday morning, I would go to the parish convent and there I would say Mass for all of the sisters, including Sister Celeste. A priest friend, Father Bill, would be there with me making sure that I went through the ritual correctly.

Even though it was a very small Mass as far as attendance was concerned, it was quite an awesome, joyful experience for me, and I did very well. This gave me confidence for the next day with its Solemn High Mass of a newly-ordained priest.

Several months before my ordination, one of Mother's sisters, Katherine, reached out to Mother in a gesture of genuine friendship. The fence that had been broken in relationship for many, many years came to life, was mended. Until that time I had never met any of Mother's relatives. Her marrying a Filipino was more than most of the family could take or tolerate. I accepted my aunt and uncle and children. So, word was out that many of my

Irish relatives would be attending my first Solemn High Mass at Sacred Heart. What a big event that would be, and especially meeting relatives that I had not known.

I got up early Sunday morning, said my extra prayers—trusting somehow that God would bless me in a special way on this very momentous occasion of my life.

The Mass, of course, in those days was said facing the church wall. I really didn't have to look at anybody, but wouldn't you know, when it came time to celebrate the Eucharist (communion), I was so nervous as I took the cup that I spilled some of the blessed wine. The sanctified wine fell on my vestment and stained it. Even though I was horrified inside, and the doubt and insecurity went rampant in my mind, the external jovial Sid let no one know, and it didn't show. I almost went crazy internally because we had been taught to be very careful of the consecrated bread and wine, for we believed that after we prayed over it, it literally was the body and blood of Jesus Christ.

After my first High Mass we retired to the convent so that the next Mass scheduled could go on uninterrupted. It was there, perhaps 300 people came for this new priest's blessing. I placed my hands on all 300—one at a time—and said a special prayer of blessing over them. I also said something personal to each one. I wanted to be sociable and relaxed. No one knew until this writing that I was terrified during those days and years of dark, disturbing self-doubts.

Nevertheless, it was a wonderful experience not only to meet my relatives, but to be able to bless them at the same time as a new priest. There was no resentment for their standoffishness. I had a beautiful time with a lot of the Irish clan that day. Even of greater joy to me was that my father was there, Justiniano Pareja Custodio.

There was a large formal reception afterwards, and to my amazement and sheer delight, there was enough money to buy a new car. That night there was a very special dinner held in my honor with a limited number of invited guests.

This is so difficult to mention—my father was not invited, and therefore did not attend the dinner. At the time I was too busy basking in all of the attention that was being bestowed upon me to even care that he was not there.

It was a custom for seminarians to go from one home to the other, milling around, congratulating their newly-ordained friends. One of my friends came to our home and found there was no party and left. I wondered about that and questioned: What's wrong? What's wrong with my family? What's wrong with me?

After my first week as a priest, seven of us decided that we would go to Carmel and have a week of just fun and pleasure. In that scenic, quiet atmosphere we golfed, ate and drank. Four years prior to the priesthood we had taken a pledge that we wouldn't drink. It wasn't a vow, it was a pledge, and it should last until five years after ordination. But some of us soon learned how to play roulette with the rules and said, "That pledge only means while in your own diocese, so if we go to Carmel or Santa Cruz, we are off-limits and can drink." And drink we did!

Then Monsignor Collins gave us two letters, one of which was in Latin and the other in English (to make sure we understood what the one in Latin said). The legal-sounding letters informed us what parishes we were assigned to as assistant pastors.

My assignment would be at St. Raphael's Parish in San Rafael of Marin County. It was a very provincial town, middle-class and upward. I was excited.

A week previous I had done a very adventurous thing. I had invited all twenty classmates over to my house for lunch made by Dad. He was a cook—and could he cook! He looked Filipino, and some might have wondered, but no one said a word. Because it was Friday we were still under the old church rule of not eating meat. Dad made tomato soup, grilled cheese sandwiches, and his own special brand of potato salad.

All the guys came and phoned their new pastors from my house. I was thrilled to have them around. Enthusiastically we asked questions back and forth. It was like all of us going out for our first assignment as Peace Corp volunteers. Our seven-room flat shook with life that happy day. It was a major event in our household. Strange how all twenty of my classmates were assembled there. Some of them I'd been with for eleven years—lived with them, laughed with them, played sports with them. There I was in their midst, caring in my unpredictable way about each of them. I'm twenty-five years of age, their colleague of many years, and not one person knows that I have a serious personal problem. No one knows I'm in mental agony and in heavy doubts . . . old Sid, the charmer, always agreeable, talks to everybody, great in football and the classroom, yet no one knew me. I didn't have a real intimate friend on earth. Yet many people cared for me. Since I was imprisoned in the trap of not sharing from fear of what self-revelation might bring, I actually blocked the intimacy that could have led to healthy mental freedom.

The first year of priesthood was supposed to be one of ecstasy, likened to a honeymoon experience.

I was picked very carefully for my first ministry because I was social and outgoing. The diocesan officials felt that I would do very well at St. Raphael's.

I thought I was something—a brand new Chevy, new clothes, new shoes, the whole works. I pulled up at the first gas station and asked, "Where's St. Raphael's Church?" What a shock as the gas station attendant said, "That's an easy one, Father, go straight a couple of blocks and then take a left." I thought, *That sounds kind of neat, being called "Father."*

It wasn't very long before I pulled up the long driveway and into an empty stall of the carport garage. The pastor there was an ex-chaplain, a former Augustinian order priest.

He wasn't originally from the San Francisco Archdiocese, and this parish was considered by priests to be a "plum." As a result, he didn't have many friends because everyone thought he got this plush parish way ahead of time, and he should have climbed the clerical ladder like everybody else, but he could not have cared less. He spent much time in quiet prayer and expected the rest of us in the parish to do the same. It was a sign of how holy one is. I was one that wasn't in the habit of spending hours in prayer. I would do my daily obligations and that was it.

All of the men in the parish rectory were very compatible. So there I was under the challenge of trying to fit in, of not making a mistake and doing exactly what I was told. By choice, again I was living an internal life of loneliness and personal torture.

Most parishioners are infatuated with the newly-ordained priest. They all want to be around you, congratulating you and being in on your first blessing. It wasn't long before I was assigned to do Sunday baptisms, give Extreme Unction, and administer the various other sacraments. After I had administered the various sacraments, I'd return to my bedroom and wonder, *Did I say the right words? Did I do the sacrament right? Did I make a mistake?* Even though during the sacramental event everything went along in a beautiful manner, it was afterwards that it would hit me and I would question everything I'd done and said. There I was—a newly-ordained priest—the toast of a highly-rated parish, and life at age twenty-five was miserable.

My first sick call was to administer to a professor from a well-known midwest university whose car had been struck on Highway 101 going toward San Francisco. As I arrived, the nurses had just placed a sheet over him since he had been pronounced dead. That was eerie to me, and the first time I had prayed over someone dead.

My worries and problems would at times get so heavy. When they did I would go to one of the first-grade classes to release my nagging tensions. With those precious, life-filled children I found temporary relief from the heaviness of my priestly life. With them I acted like a kid as I taught them. It kept my sanity just as holding Sister Celeste's hand did. These children were now my link to sanity.

After I had been at the parish for about three months, I had my first bout with mental and physical exhaustion—which would be the first of a series of mounting events that would lead to an eventual nervous breakdown. One afternoon on a very warm day I found myself sweating, perspiring profusely, and then I would break out in chills. Constantly, day after day, I would feel nauseous, sick and weak. There was absolutely no energy left in me to carry on my ordinary parish duties.

Father Dan, one of the prison chaplains, came to me one day and said, "Sid, you must go to bed." He gave me a great big "hot toddy," and put me to bed to sweat it out, but it did no good. After resting I felt the same—exhausted. Here I was only twenty-five years old and already beginning my skid downward. I was wound up like a rubber band that was ready to snap. Every baptism, every anointing, every little hospital visit was done in fear and worry. Yet, apparently, no one recognized the seriousness of my condition. I was friendly to everybody, laughing, putting on a very confident front.

It was evident that several of the nurses at one of the hospitals thought much of me. The respect and feeling was mutual. One night I was making a last-minute hospital check on my day off, perhaps it was as late as eleven o'clock. One of the nurses came running down the hall and said, "Father Sid, Father Sid, rush to Room 109. One of the nurses is dying and she needs you right now."

I rushed into the room. There was one of my favorite nurses on a cot, apparently near death. I began to prepare to administer the Last Rites to her when all of a sudden she sat straight up and yelled, "Surprise!" along with a host of other nurses. The lights went on. In came a candle-lit cake for my birthday. I loved the surprise party, the singing and the momentary merriment.

8

Pending Mental Disaster

To this point of my life I had not had one personal God-centered experience. God was a distant force that I had never reached, or touched, or sensed, or experienced. No wonder I was so desperately restless, bothered, empty, hungry.

The simple, wise words of Saint Augustine were in my passive memory, but they were not ringing out for me to hear and understand: "Our hearts are restless, O Lord, until they rest in You."

In the midst of all this confusion, I had met a person who told me that he was a born-again Christian, a Protestant. He had heard me speaking and said, "Father Sid, don't you know that Jesus Christ is the only priest?"

For a moment that statement jolted me, but I thought, *This Protestant doesn't know any more than I do,* and put it out of my mind.

My daily life was plagued by Canonical (church) rules—and it seemed endless—every waking hour was consumed with obeying these bombarding rules. I tried to get exhausted doing countless activities, thinking that I could then sleep. I would retire only to worry if there was a sin that I had not confessed, a sacrament I had done wrong, or if I had brought displeasure to Father O'Malley or anyone else. As a result, during my first year at the parish I missed only one day of parish duty. In fact, I only took off one-half day of work. That was the day I canceled my appointments and phoned my former confessor at the seminary.

Father J. B. Quinlan was a small-framed man. When I arrived at the seminary he invited me into his office and said, "Well, Sid, how's it going at your new parish? Are you finding everything satisfactory? What do you think of the priesthood now that your first year is drawing to a close?"

"Father, that's exactly why I am here. I do not believe that I am even ordained."

He looked at me somewhat startled with questioning eyes and said, "Sid, don't be ridiculous, what do you mean you don't think you were ordained? I was there and you were there and you're a priest."

"Father, let me explain," and I went into great detail about the former hidden sins of impurity, not feeling the presence of God, and the doubt I had about whether there was really sufficient commitment on my part during the ordination ceremony. I related that I didn't know God in any personal relationship.

He looked at me and said, "Sid, get a hold on yourself. Be a man. Go back to the parish and get to work—think of others and not of yourself. Now get out of here and go with God."

As I walked down the sidewalk to my car I was so dejected and felt so alone, grieved that no one seemed to understand the seriousness of my internal situation. No one seemed to understand—not even God!

When I got back to the parish, Father Dan, one of the chaplains from San Quentin happened to be in the parlor alone. I asked, "Father Dan, could I talk to you for a moment?"

"Certainly, Sid, sit down."

I told him of my fears and my problems and my anxieties. His remark scared me more than all the other problems that I was going through. "Sid," he said, "perhaps you should see a psychiatrist."

"A psychiatrist!" I exclaimed. "Why on earth would I need a psychiatrist? Never, never!"

Dan looked at me in gentleness and said, "Yes, Sid, I think you ought to take a couple of days off and see a psychiatrist and get a hold of the problem that you are facing." He had spotted my torment and was trying to deal with what the others had ignored.

I thanked him and retired to my quarters. I knew I would simply have to ignore his advice and go on. Slowly, during my first year of parish ministry the storm clouds of pending mental disaster were gathering and even becoming detectable.

I had a beautiful suite of rooms. However, of the four of us living in the house, there was no relationship between any of us. I don't wish to condemn them, but there just wasn't any closeness and sharing intimacy. We were free, of course, as adult priests to come and go and to enter anyone's room that we wanted to, but there was nothing between us. We never even got together to pray. However, before dinner we gathered around Pastor George, and even though I was pledged officially not to drink for five years, they were always offering me a beer and saying, "Go ahead and have one, Sid, that really isn't drinking." Father George was rather tough on this. Even though he swore and had his holy hour, he wanted the rules obeyed to the letter—explicitly.

Father George depended on me very heavily. Every afternoon I drove him and his dog around the hills and the lake. A famous expression around the house was, "Sid, Sid, where is Sid?" It started getting to me, and I would take off going for walks, going for solitary drives just to be away from him.

Father George insisted that we all be in by 11:00 P.M. It was a standing joke around the parish and diocese that even the teenagers could be out until twelve, and here we were grown men who had to be in by eleven.

I had a deep hunger for a friend, one whom I could share with and love—yet I dared not dwell on that need. I dared not think about what it meant to be lonely or what was missing in my life. Therefore, it was busy, busy, busy, busy. Every moment of every day and night would be in business so that I would not have thinking time.

The priests and lay people alike all seemed to like me. I was all things to all people. I tried never to upset anyone. Father O'Malley was the only one that I seemed to upset—he was seeing what Sid wasn't. When he wanted me and I wasn't there, believe you me, in no uncertain terms, he let me know.

While in the minor seminary, Tom Coleman, a priest, was one of my big brothers. He had sent a letter to the Catholic Department of Education recommending that they ask me to teach. Most of the high school teachers in the diocese were Jesuits, but at this time the diocesan priests were beginning to teach also. There was quite a bit of debate going on that we should not get into teaching and remain simply parish priests.

I went to Father Dan to see what he would think of the possibility. (This is the priest who had asked me to see a psychiatrist.) After I explained the letter he looked at me and said, "Well, Sid, if that's what you want, it might be good for you. It could be the thing that you are seeking." I thanked him for listening and left.

I went to see Monsignor Bradley, full of fear and apprehension. He asked basically two simple questions: Did I like books, and did I like kids?

I replied that I loved to read, and yes, I loved kids.

They were in desperate need at that time for priest teachers. After my interview it was only a matter of moments until I was accepted to teach at a co-educational high school in Oakland: Bishop O'Dowd High School. There were about 1,000 students and they were the cream of the crop. The average I.Q. of a student there was 114. I was assigned to teach three classes of boys, and two of girls. I took to teaching like a duck to water.

My worries about the sacraments were now lessened because I was no longer acting as the parish priest but as a teacher.

With my taking the teaching position, of course, it required my moving. I lived with an easy-going Portuguese priest, Dominic Carerea. He had a deep, deep voice. It was a tradition in that house to always have a drink before dinner. Of course, he wasn't against my drinking at all. The first time he asked me, "Sid, would you like a martini?" I replied, "Yes, I would, but what is it?"

"Well, we just call it Dominic's Famous Martini, or simply 'Dominic's Double.'"

For the first several days it was just one. Then it was two or three, and some times I could barely get down to dinner!

9

Bishop O'Dowd High School

I loved school. I loved the students and they seemed to want me to share in their festivities. I was invited to some of their private parties. I would chaperone at the dances, and it was interesting how some of the girls would ask "Father Sid" to dance. I would just have a ball. It was their way of expressing friendliness to me, and I was beginning to experience what it meant to converse and to share with people.

I was teaching a class in public speaking. One of my pupils, an Italian girl, really excelled in the class. It became apparent that she was a candidate to be entered in a national contest for public speaking: The Voice of Democracy Contest. She had prepared a five-minute speech on democracy. She was the State of California winner! It was then a trip to Washington, D.C.

Of course, I had to get permission from the Bishop to attend. He told me that I couldn't miss any school time. Since the students were having a retreat for three days, I was able to go with Judy and her father.

The announcement of the four National Winners was going to be held at the foot of the Washington Monument on February 22. It was there I saw J. F. Kennedy. I had spoken to him about a half hour earlier. Later when he passed, I said, "Hi, Senator," he just looked at me and said nothing. What a disappointment because I was sure that I would have gotten at least a "Good morning, Father."

From all reports, we understood that Judy was now one of the top twelve finalists.

Senator Kennedy then got up and announced Judy's name first. Her father and I nearly went insane with excitement. Truly, that was an exhilarating highlight of my early teaching years—my first year of teaching and coaching. A National Speech Winner among a half million participating students! Judy's father wanted to treat Judy and me for the joyous victory. "What would you enjoy for a special celebration?"

Judy quickly answered: "A trip to New York City."

We took a whirlwind tour to New York. We got there at midnight and had five hours to see the city. We rented a car, saw all of the large well-known buildings, and ate breakfast at "Lindy's" at two in the morning. I took off my Roman collar and they introduced me as "The senator from California." What an imaginary fun-filled world it was for all those precious moments. I called back to Oakland and asked if I could have another day. The principal told me to get back and get back quick! He had already given me one more day than the Archbishop had approved.

When we arrived in Oakland the mayor was there to greet us. There was even a parade of many cars, many students, and many dignitaries. Judy and the school received a special commendation from the Mayor of Oakland. Later, commendations from the Legislature arrived for Judy and Bishop O'Dowd School.

I was in "seventh heaven," and yet I was still going through all this internal and mental turmoil.

In May, after I'd taught about eight months, one day my hands started shaking during Mass. I couldn't control my nerves. I was thinking, *Oh no. I'm having a heart attack!*

I was in love with everything I was doing, but the doctor said, "Two weeks, Father Sid, in Arizona to relax." Of course, I only laughed and ignored his recommendation.

I was having many sleepless nights. So I returned to the doctor. He gave me pills so that I could sleep. They worked for a while, but it didn't last.

I had been assigned to drive four students to school each day. I was afraid to tell anyone of my two or three bouts with shaking. I was afraid that they would take the privilege of teaching away from me. I became really concerned when I started shaking almost uncontrollably while driving a car with the four students in it.

Most of my classes were taught on the second floor. There were times I would be so faint that I could hardly make my way down to the first floor. I would wait until the students were in the cafeteria, then I would grab the hand rail of the stairway and struggle down the steps—clinging at times to the railing so as not to tumble down the stairs. Here I am, twenty-six years old, a previous athlete and nearly entirely physically and mentally broken. Somehow I'd manage to get through one day and begin the next and try to get through that. I'd smile bigger than ever. I barely made it through the end of the school year—but make it I did.

Two of my friends from minor seminary days were going to be ordained, and one of them asked me to stand with him at his first Mass. What a thrill it was to be asked. I wanted to go, but I didn't know if I could make it. I told him I would be glad to go, and as always, Sid was a little late.

How can a priest be late for such an important Mass? I got there just a moment before the Mass began. I could tell Jim was really upset. Somehow my mind was gone. I don't remember participating in the Mass. I didn't remember going to his party. My mind simply was not there. I was now well into the maze of my first mental breakdown and didn't realize what was happening. I called it exhaustion. Now they call it burn-out, and I was only twenty-six!

My first teaching year was one of work, work, work. I guess you could say I was a work-a-holic. Even though I was exhausted, I had a wonderful year; the kids loving me and me loving the kids. Oh, if I only could have trusted God to put me together, but I didn't even know God. I still had no personal God. I was keeping everything a secret.

To make matters worse, I had to go to summer school to get teaching credentials. I didn't realize when I entered summer school that it was going to be a blessing. It was there I met Brother Patrick and his buddy, Brother Killian. Both were big, husky, and athletic-looking. Pat looked just like a movie star. We began running around the track, played all sorts of sports, sat around, talked and drank beer. Somehow with the mixture of all of these I seemed to get over my first burn-out. I studied and did very well.

All through the summer I was on librium, which is a tranquilizer, and that seemed to help. By the time vacation was over and school was to begin, I thought I was physically and mentally "A-OK."

Just before school was to begin, word came from the Bishop that I would remain teaching at the same high school, but they were going to move me to another parish quarters. This was the beginning of the "system" playing checkers with me. I didn't know it at the time, but it was the first of many, many moves.

I was angry as I moved into a house where the priest was all alone—a reformed drinker. So I threw myself even more into the activities of school. How I missed that other parish!

At this new house the priest and I never talked. We just co-existed. Suddenly he was moved and another priest, Father Matthew

O'Conner, was moved into the house as a temporary pastor. We at least talked. Father Matt nevertheless did have a wonderful sense of humor. I fondly remember many laughing moments as he mimicked with great artistry. We did not communicate to any depth, however. We never had dinner together. Again, he soon moved, and we never knew each other. I really didn't care. I was becoming a part of that system where you just never had sharing friends.

One night I was acting like a kid at school (as I think about it now it was because I never lived a teenage life). Some of us from the Teen Club, which I sponsored, were going bowling (Frank, Jim, Rochdle and Father Sid). We stopped at the corner and up came this big basketball player, George Gardner, and he had his girl with him. She was holding her baby sister in her lap. All of a sudden George gunned his engine a little and said to me, "Want to race, Father?"

I couldn't resist. Something in me just snapped. I knew I had to race that kid down McArthur Boulevard. So I gunned my engine and off we peeled—leaving black marks behind us with tires screeching. As suddenly as I heard the noise and I was winning, I saw two flashing red lights behind us. Then I saw two motor bike cops pull up. They pulled us over.

There had been a crackdown in Oakland on speeding, and if it was an adult they automatically went to jail. You can imagine my embarrassment when the cop came up, looked in the window and asked questioningly,

"You're the priest? You have got to be kidding! What's your name?"

"Sir, my name is Father Custodio. I'm a teacher at Bishop O'Dowd Catholic High School."

At that the policeman looked at me totally amazed and again said, "You are a what? At a what? I thought a priest takes a vow to save humanity, not slaughter them on the highways. You should be ashamed of yourself." At that, he pulled out the black pad for tickets and wrote one up for me. I sat there embarrassed, and for a long time so ashamed that I couldn't open my mouth.

The policeman let George drive away. When I started my car the law officer said, "Father, I think you'd better wait here. I don't want you to be tempted beyond your capacity. So help me, if I ever catch you drag racing your students again, priest or no priest, you are going to end up behind bars."

At that, I drove slowly away—with many hours ahead not only to ponder my ticket, but why that childish drive was coming out of me.

The next day as I drove in to the school many of the kids were lining the driveway, and as I'd go past they'd all make the sound of a revved-up engine and laugh. It was all over the school that Father Custodio had been caught dragging. As I got to the home room and was writing the announcements on the blackboard for the day, the students behind me were revving their "mouth" engines at every word I had written. Then they made the familiar siren sounds of pursuing police. I turned about and said, "That's right, guys, I did it. I did it, but you want to know something? It was exciting AND stupid, but I learned my lesson. I'm telling you one thing, I'll never do it again."

My time with the students was one of constant exhilaration and kept me from going over the deep end.

At the end of my second school year I got another infamous letter. It was the same type I would get year after year. I was told I would be moved to another high school across the bay in San Mateo. It was an all-boys school, with an approximate enrollment of 1,000 students— Serra High School. When I received the notice of my change to another high school, I strongly demanded an answer to my question, "Why am I being switched to another school after only two years at Bishop O'Dowd School?"

The reason given for being moved again was that Father Fred Hanley, a former big brother of mine in the seminary, was going to move to Washington, D.C., to be groomed for a higher position in the church (I presumed correctly). Because he taught the subjects that I could teach, they wanted me to replace him. They were trying to make my change look like a real honor, but I was torn because now I had gotten to know and love the O'Dowd kids. Here I was being transferred again. It would be a whole new set of problems, students—and I didn't like it.

10

Making a Cursillo

When I arrived at my new parish, St. Gregory's in San Mateo, I decided to take a walk down to the high school where I was going to teach. It was only eight blocks from my new parish home. As I was walking through the parish school yard, I noticed a very attractive woman walking between classrooms. This young woman, obviously in her twenties, was very beautiful and very attractive. I approached her and introduced myself: "I'm Father Sid, the new priest here, who will be teaching at Serra High School."

With reserve she introduced herself: "I'm Pamela Stevens, the new third-grade teacher here."

After that simple introduction, a few moments in duration, something inside me clicked. When I left I asked her if we could meet again and talk. With less reserve, Pamela answered, "Yes, I would like that."

Most of our meetings were in Pam's classroom, or we'd go on short trips, but there was always another person with us. There had to be a chaperon. Marie O'Dell, Pam's roommate, whom I liked very much, was the one we picked to go with us.

Eventually, Pam and I started holding hands. Then it turned into kissing, lip to lip. I am twenty-eight years old, and it's the first time I had ever kissed a woman in this way. It felt so good that my whole body began to vibrate. It began sounding like a heart and ended with drums banging. Suddenly I realized that I was lusting. I had to go to confession before I said Mass the next day, for I knew I'd committed a mortal sin. Now fear was back and also the mental attacks. Whether or not my heart was in love, I could not say, but I knew my body was, and that was sin to me.

I began to go to an Irish priest that didn't know any of us diocesan priests personally. You could ring a bell, tell your confession, and the priest never saw you.

I always had to be "clean" before I said Mass. I never went to the pulpit without telling God I was sorry. So in reality I was living a Jekyll-and-Hyde life, and most of it was mental.

During those days, priests could confess directly to God only in cases of emergencies. Otherwise, it always had to be to another priest. If you were caught, you could always talk to God, but then as soon as you had the time you had to go to a priest to make the confession complete.

One time when Pam and I ended up in a tight book closet and I fondled her momentarily, I thought she was going to faint in my arms. I thought to myself, *Oh, my God, what have I done?*

The next Sunday I had been called to do

some parish Baptisms, and all my past hang-ups hit me with a renewed fury. Even though I said the words very distinctly and slowly to make sure every syllable of the sacramental words were clear and distinct, and even have innocent fun with the parents of the babies and make them feel at home in the church, I would inwardly panic, wondering if I did it wrong.

Pamela was one person with whom I could share my fears.

One thing I knew for certain—that my passions were becoming uncontrollable. But God intervened at the end of our third year at San Mateo. Pamela decided to move to Denver, Colorado, to be nearer her parents and family.

I was devastated. I missed her and she missed me. Now my body knew what it was to feel touched by a woman's lips. To cope with my loneliness, I was drinking heavier and heavier. I'm drinking bourbon on the rocks one after another and often. I looked forward to any social event so that I could hold a woman in my arms and dance, and every chance I'd get I'd give one a kiss.

My life now seemed to be a series of nightmares, fantasies, and having all these strange relationships in the parish. I was attracted to almost every woman I saw. I didn't make advances or touch them, but I was attracted to them.

Right after the Christmas holiday something was going to take place in my life that would crash my world of drinking and touching and fantasizing for women. This was called "Making a Cursillo"—a Spanish term for a short course. Actually, it was going to be an INTENSIVE course in Christianity.

A layman, Jim Carlson, was one of the speakers, along with a blind Franciscan priest. Then it struck me: How can a "layman" say anything authoritatively about Jesus?

During these three days I listened as the men shared what Christ meant to them. After every talk we would sit around, nine to a table, and discuss what we'd heard. Then we'd draw pictures. At first I thought this was so ridiculous—grown men drawing pictures and coloring them. Later I got a real kick out of drawing the pictures and coloring them.

After a full day of talking about faith and Jesus, it wasn't long until we were laughing, singing, and great amounts of joy flooded into our hearts and overflowed everywhere.

The second day all the talks were about love and how Christ Jesus, the Person, can meet us in the sacraments. Here I am sitting there, all I had cared about was, did I say the right words at every sacrament! Now I'm hearing that Jesus Christ can meet us there so we can have a personal encounter with Him. It was blowing me away! We are not drawing now, we're sitting up, listening, singing, and even a few of us are being hugged. This was all new, and I couldn't quite relate to what was happening.

Then the Franciscan priest who was blind got up to speak. He spoke on the prodigal son. How my heart melted toward him as I heard him speak. After he finished I sat there silently and in tears. A little later I asked him if he would hear my confession.

I told him all about my sins, about the women and the drink. He had such unbelievable compassion on me. He told me again how Jesus was the one that forgave abundantly. That was a major step, the trigger for my revealing the innermost secret parts of the complicated me to that simple and yet profound blind priest.

All of the men leaders shared from their experiences how Christ was the major part, the center of their lives. One expression that stuck with me, and always will be a part of me: "Jesus Christ and I are an overwhelming majority."

By this time, I'd been a priest for nine years and I was just starting to get excited as they mentioned Jesus Christ and the Word of God. There were three basic things shared with us that we had to do. They were in this order: STUDY the Word of God; PRAYER time with Jesus Christ; and then LABOR for Him. These are essentials for every Christian that wants to stay in constant touch with God and grow in his Christian experience. It had to be a daily Christian TALK *and* WALK.

Up to now, all I had done was study and pray out of my prayer books. They were never prayers that were made up on my own. They were never a personal meeting with a loving, powerful Jesus Christ.

On the second day we were asked the question: If you had four or five hours on a

Saturday afternoon and all the money you needed, no commitments, nothing that stood in your way, what would you do with that time?

Here I was a Catholic priest and I wrote: "I'd put on a lively musical."

I was given a Bible at the Cursillo. I acted as if I had never owned one before. We were going to use it now each day to study from it in order to develop our Christian life. What an experience that was—to open God's Book and hear from Him directly, what He had to say, person to person—God to ME!

On Saturday night by candlelight we shared the Eucharist together. There were many visitors that came, laymen and priests that had already made the Cursillo weekend. All the music that came from their lips was praise and thanksgiving to a living, risen Christ. They were hugging and sharing. The men had joy and peace shining right out of their eyes. For me, the cold planet earth was crumbling. The new and authentic Christian world was unfolding and touching me, love-hungry me.

The next morning about six o'clock, while one is still nearly asleep, there were perhaps a hundred voices that came into the dormitory singing in Spanish, "We welcome you in the morning." They sang to us, hugged us. There was such joy emitting from these men. As they hugged me and prayed for me I stood there with tears streaming down my cheeks for I had never known such love. There was such laughter. I had never seen men laugh so hard—unless it had been the result of dirty jokes, but everything here was clean and refreshing. We went from laughing to crying. I thought: *What's next?* Then we all participated in Mass. The visitors left and we started the last day of our talks. We talked, discussed, drew pictures and colored them. We put them on the walls of the room so everyone could see what the group was experiencing.

One of the most interesting, awesome, terrifying and blessed moments of the entire Cursillo was what we called "walking the gauntlet of hugs." There were perhaps forty men that formed a line and you walked by them and each blessed you and gave you a hug.

Before me in line was one of the most famous preachers of the Bay Area, a handsome, debonair man noted also as the best clerical comedian. It was interesting as I watched him go toward the line. The first guy that hugged him startled him so that his back arched. It was as if he simply could not handle it—this genuine Christian caring, man to man.

As each man hugged he said, "De Colores," which is a song title meaning "many colors." More significantly, the Spanish greeting wishes you a joyful, love-filled Christian journey.

I thought it would be simple for me, but I'd never been hugged by a man before this. For some reason I was ready to be blessed, to be loved. I could just be myself—plain, simple, Sid.

Then came the time to have the last meeting of our intensive Christian experience. I knew I felt wonderful. I didn't know exactly what was happening, but I had been touched deeply and had very little to say. As we were about to leave we were asked to go to the dining room for a final talk, and there were two hundred or more people there welcoming us into this newer Christian community. All of them had been through the Cursillo course—not only men, but their wives and their families.

It's an open meeting now and anyone who wants to can stand up and talk and share what Jesus Christ has done in his life. What a difference because on the first night they asked us to all stand and identify ourselves. I'd gotten up, "I'm Sid, a public-speaking teacher," and talked and rambled for six minutes. I was only supposed to tell my name.

Now it was Sunday. The Spirit of God had worked in my heart. As I shared I said, "I'm Father Sid, as some of you know." At that several priests began laughing. I suppose now they were expecting a two-hour sermon. Then I continued, "And I've fallen in love with a lot of guys that have been here this weekend. I think somehow I've fallen in love with Jesus Christ." With that I shut up and sat down. I didn't know why, but everyone clapped. I hadn't given any punch line, but what I said for the first time in my life I believe was from my heart instead of my head. That three days was going to be the beginning of one of the biggest journeys of my life.

Yes, I knew about Jesus. I knew about His

resurrection just as I had known ABOUT President Eisenhower, President Lincoln, and President Washington, but I had never met any of them nor had I met Jesus Christ. The Scripture tells us, "To the thirsty one, I will give water, without price from the fountain of the water of life." God had made a promise. That promise was a free gift, a gift of life, life without price simply because He loves us.

According to John 3:16, God loved me so much that He gave His only Son, Jesus, that if I, Sid, would believe in Him, I would not perish, but I would have eternal life. I learned that I could know God in a personal way through His Son, Jesus, that He was reaching out to me, desiring me to come to Him through Jesus. At last, I knew that God had made the provision that I could have a relationship with Him.

Then I knew what it was like to have new life, and understood more of what Jesus had said to John: "I came so that they might have life and have it more abundantly."

I left the weekend with my heart full to overflowing, and my drive back to the parish was one of real blessing. Also, I had made some very strong decisions. One was that I would not drink for a year. I wanted to be free of the alcohol. I was laughing to myself as I parked my car. It was New Year's Eve and Sid wasn't going to drink a drop.

Most priests that I knew enjoyed a drink before they sat down to eat. The parish I was in at the time had two assistants, and one, of course, was the priest that had seen me come in "under-the-influence" several times. I stood in the rectory hallway wondering, *What am I going to do when they ask me to have a drink this "special" New Year's Eve?* I knew for sure that I wasn't going to take one no matter what they said. Finally, I went into the living room and said, "Hi, guys." Oh how I wanted to give each of them a hug and share with them the blessings that I had just been through the past 72 hours.

Frank looked at me and asked, "Want a drink, Sid?"

"No, thanks, Frank."

No one commented. I sat down. For the first time I didn't feel I had to talk. They didn't even tease me, but I sensed that they were looking at me very intensely—waiting for this guy who always talks so much to say something! They knew that I would never let silence prevail in any room for more than a few seconds. Somehow I had thought that silence should not be . . . even if I didn't know what to talk about, I said something. Now I was going to sit and listen. How I wanted to tell each of those men that I had come in contact with the Person of Jesus Christ. The New Year entered and found me very quiet, very sober and very happy.

11

Tenth Year in Summer School

Even though I knew Jesus as my personal Savior, I did not know Him as Lord. He was more of a powerful personal force in nourishing a group of people. So I threw all my efforts into building Christian community. It was community, community, community. Cursillo did push community with its source in Jesus, but I jumped into community, being a people-centered person rather than jumping into Scripture and Jesus.

It seemed I could do nothing right. There I was somewhat free in spirit and I'd tell the men of the parish who were standing in the back of the church, "Come on, people. Let's be near each other; take a seat anywhere up near the altar. Let's celebrate the Mass as Christian brothers. Let's make our parish a Christian community."

From the looks I saw on a number of faces, I could see that the parish people thought I had gone totally berserk. Yet, I thought for the first time in my life that I was acting normal. Life balance for me was still some distance away. With the wonderful experience that I had had from Cursillo I was fulfilled. Even my body was happy. There was little lust, and I did not even have a glass of liquor touch my lips for over eleven months. The Cursillo experience had affected me: body, soul, and spirit. Yet, I was acting very childish. Actually, more like a baby. I had no Christian fellowship to nurture and direct my Christian growth. I was like a baby left on a doorstep. Jesus was not yet fully real in my personal life and in my relationships.

In the Book of Genesis (Chapter 2:18) God says to us clearly: "It is not good for man to live alone. I will make a suitable companion to help him." This simple, direct comment on human reality somehow had never reached my personal awareness, nor my theology for healthy Christian living. It would be a number of years after my Cursillo that God's loving grace would penetrate my confused mind and hungry heart with the realization that I needed both a God of love and a constant, particular companion for personal health, growth and success.

Our house was entirely different. It had to be absolutely proper and according to the law. Our new pastor was a fanatic about being on time, rather than just being punctual. How I cried out for acceptance from the Monsignor who had been the superintendent who invited me into the teaching profession.

A blessing it was when several of us, lay persons and I, put on "The Wizard of Oz" with our parish eighth-grade students. The new pastor said, not directly to me but to one of the other priests, "That was a very professional production." That was all I wanted to hear: "You're doing a fine job." Somehow most men in the priestly profession at that time did not praise or compliment one another.

I'm trying wholeheartedly to teach the message and happiness of the Cursillo throughout my parish. I decided then that now was the time for me to leave my high school teaching work to become an assistant pastor of a flock, so I went to my superior and said, "Monsignor, I want to leave teaching and go back to parish work."

"Sid, we're going to have a State evaluation this year. You've been with us here in San Mateo seven years and have been teaching nine years. I'd like to keep all the veterans we can during this evaluation year. Please, can you not give us another year?"

I pondered his question for a moment, then replied, "I suppose so, Monsignor, but for my final year in teaching I want to move to another parish. There are two important reasons, and I want to move NOW, so you give me a trade-off."

It took him a while, but finally he said, "All right, Sid, what do you want?"

"I want to move from St. Gregory. First, to get away from the new pastor and the military regime. Second, to get away from the occasion of sin. I don't want to fall into my drinking pattern again."

"That sounds reasonable. Where would you like to go?"

"St. James Parish."

I then phoned Father Frank, the guy I loved from afar, even though we lived eight feet from each other's suite of rooms. I told him that I was asking to leave St. Gregory's and teaching, and that I'd asked to go to St. James' community.

"Sid," said Frank, "you won't be happy there. I know you won't. If I were you I would try Immaculate Heart Parish in Belmont—it's only a suggestion."

I thanked him, hung up the phone. I got the Superintendent on the phone again and asked if he'd processed my request. I told him I had changed my mind and wanted to go to the Belmont Parish rather than to St. James.

He replied, "Okay, Sid, I'll let you go to Immaculate Heart."

For the tenth year in succession, I decided to go to summer school. The Second Vatican Council (1964) had just been held and Pope John XXIII had made the statement that he was opening the proverbial windows and doors and letting fresh air in via the Holy Spirit. We were given opportunity to take a theology course on the happenings of the Vatican Council, so I signed up.

We heard points on the draft that would come out later to the Catholic people throughout the world as official teachings. The draft basically consisted of four major steps in the renewal process of the Roman Catholic Church: **Self-Awareness, Self-Reform, Reunion** with all other Christians, and **Dialogue** with the modern world.

I was especially enthused that the Catholic Church I served was reaching out to other Christians in a very different approach. The renewal, at last, was trying to have a reunion with other Christians rather than demanding that they return like lost sheep to the Catholic Church, coming back into the fold, so to speak. I didn't understand much of this at the time, but it sounded good and important.

The topic I chose for writing my final paper for the summer class was: "Jesus Christ, the Resurrected One!" Here I had been a priest for ten years and I was just beginning to meet Jesus and His power-filled life after death. I felt strongly that I was being called to a new life of total surrender. Father Gregory kept saying to us over and over: "We are called. We are called to total surrender by Jesus—total surrender."

For the life of me I couldn't figure out what the teacher meant by "total surrender to Jesus." He kept using the term that Jesus must be the Lord of our lives, that we must be led by the Spirit of the living Christ, and that we should meditate upon the Word of God, because the Word was living and sharper than a two-edged sword and it could change our lives.

I pondered, *How can the Word change our lives?*

That friendship-filled summer of study and play was a major turning point in my love-hungry and fear-filled life. That special summer of liberating theology, coupled with the Cursillo spirit of love that I had experienced six months earlier, would unleash enormous repressed feelings. It released an unharnessed personal energy that would push me eventually to near destruction.

12

Heading for a Crash

In my first year at my new parish at Belmont, California, I had my students do some writing in the English class. They were to draw pictures of grammar things and tell me about the pictures. This approach flowed from my Cursillo experience and the summer school impact on my life. Soon I heard some of the faculty say, "Who's that nut teaching English by having the students drawing pictures, coloring—and loving it, and even talking about learning more English?" This method was making an impact.

During the Thanksgiving weekend my brother Ed and I flew to the University of Southern California game with Notre Dame. Notre Dame was undefeated. As we were flying, I was having an attack of choking. I became terrified, for it reminded me of what I had gone through when I began my first burnout while teaching at O'Dowd High School, nine years earlier. Somewhere I had a leftover tranquilizer pill in my pocket. I took it, but felt very jittery and terribly boxed-in during the flight.

The night before the USC game, I went to a

people-filled pre-game party. It was a real bash.
I met a fellow San Francisco priest, Jimmy O.,
at the noisy celebration. I joined his party and
tried bringing the GOOD NEWS of community
and sharing with them.

I had some of the GOOD NEWS of Jesus
Christ in me, however, without a real, personal
relationship and commitment to Him and His
values. I was like an extroverted Christian
without the necessary inner deep connection
and relationship.

When we got back my brother Ed and I
decided to go to Tahoe for a couple of days. Ed
wanted to stay, so I drove back alone. The trip
wasn't very long, but I became so tired I was
getting somewhat delirious. I stopped in Sacramento for coffee, not knowing whether or not
I could drive another mile. It seemed to wake
me up, but somehow energy was draining from
my body. I was burning out in my head, but I
didn't recognize the severity of the symptoms.

I kept driving in that unhealthy condition
of mind because I had a date the next morning
with the three Christian brothers and Kay, my
summer school friends. The date was to be an
all-day picnic in the Russian River area. The
mental imbalance and nervous exuberance
were again dangerously leading my life.

I got to the entrance of the San Francisco
Bay Bridge and paused for a moment, trying to
decide if I should go across the bridge or not.
Halfway across the bridge I began to shake
almost uncontrollably. Then I heard a voice. It
was like all the banchees of hell were screaming
at me: "Run into the bridge. Jam the car into

the bridge. Ram the bridge. Ram the bridge."

I screamed aloud, "No! No! No! I won't do it. I won't do it." Something inside of me said, "Fight, Sid, fight."

Again I heard the screams: "Hit the bridge. End it all. End it, Sid. End it."

I was screaming, praying and crying, not knowing what to do. I was thinking perhaps I should end it all right now—thirty-six crazy roller coaster years. Why not? I'll probably never amount to much anyway. Finally, I got to the other side of the bridge, and parked at a side street. I sat there full of torment and restlessness. I had no peace.

Somehow I managed to get to Joe O'Brien's place, slept briefly, and took my friends on the picnic.

The following Sunday I had no energy to say Mass. To calm my nerves I drank a little. The next day I ended up in the hospital with fluid in my lungs.

When I left Belmont and teaching in June, 1965, there was no "Thank you"—nothing. It was as though I was simply going to move from square 1 to square 2 of the chess board. I'm nearing the age of forty, and feel I'm going no place. I feel like a zero. I not only felt like a zero, but the church and educational leaders made that zero feeling even deeper. There was never any expression of gratitude or appreciation by those in the official positions. This would be an inhuman lack in a secular or money-hungry organization. Here I was working in a Christian organization. My leaders often gave little or no thanks. Surely it must have been a mere oversight on some people's part. Nevertheless that oversight is tragic and destructive in people's lives—my life, in that instance.

Without any farewell, thank-you dinner from my colleagues or superiors, I embarked on my new venture, a parish priest again, only now one with much teaching experience, and with new, revolutionary theology of the people of God on the move toward love and social justice.

I had more zeal than sense going into the new parish, St. Patrick's in San Jose, California. I wanted to love everybody, touch everybody, hug everybody. I wanted to tell everybody that Jesus Christ is a resurrected Christ in the vague way that I understood Him.

I wasn't at the new parish very long until I formed a little community. My team consisted of five open-minded nuns, a former seminarian, Ron, and several lay people. We were being nourished by each other, and by what I'd learned at the Cursillo and summer school, but not by the dynamic Word of God. I was living someone else's testimony, and now these people were living on my testimony. I decided I would try to teach them in an adult Bible class.

One afternoon the pastor came to me and asked, "Sid, what are you giving adult Catholic classes for? These people are already Catholics. That isn't at all necessary." I had already heard by the grapevine that he was very upset with me.

One Sunday morning while I was in the

pulpit teaching, the pastor went on a war path. He came behind the pulpit (hidden from the congregation) and pounded on the wall saying to me, "Get out of that pulpit. Get out of that pulpit."

Even though he could not be seen by the parishioners, they heard the pounding, and I knew that I was in trouble. This type of pastor and assistant pastor relationship (or non-relationship) continued for several months. At Christmas time the pastor got word that he was being moved. This was strange, indeed, because the normal church procedure was when there was a conflict or trouble, the pastor stayed and those under him were moved. In this remarkable turn of events, they moved the pastor.

A new pastor came. I'd gone to him after my Cursillo experience and confessed some of my problems, and now here he came, knowing full well what I'd confessed to him. When I actually told Father Red my personal problems he shocked me like a lightning bolt with his remark: "Sid, sometimes the priestly pressures and other circumstances cause a few padres to go on alcoholic binges—sometimes even to an experience of sexual intercourse."

At the time I was part teenager and part adult because I was shocked—thrown into a mental tailspin. Perhaps Father Red used the shock treatment deliberately, for I didn't crucify myself as badly about my sins from that time on.

To my surprise, he quickly and genuinely liked me, and went along with me on bringing the Christian community together. He even presided at the graduation celebrations when the Catholics graduated from their adult-formation theology classes.

Mary Jane, the principal of the school, became a close friend, and helped me so much. One night I put a candle in the rectory window. She, too, had one in her window across the way, and I knew she was thinking and praying for me. I needed her friendly thoughts and daily prayers.

I was engaged, full tilt, with the challenge of bringing the "new theology" (which is basically the genuine, original Good News of Jesus Christ) to the mixed population of San Jose. It was heavily Anglo, and growing more Latino each week.

In the midst of my daily, full-scheduled, clerical outreach, Mary Jane, with her quiet friendship, was an authentic, refreshing oasis—at times, a genuine mind saver and life saver. It wasn't "friendship-at-first-sight," for us. She was a principal with much parish authority; I was yet basically a stubborn relentless rebel—albeit with a high mixture of Filipino charm. We never clashed, never argued. Yet there was, at first, a reserve between us that prevented friendship. There came an event that broke the cool, respectful reserve. This breakthrough led to one of the friendships that I cherish most in my life.

Mary Jane was ill and confined to her bed. An ear problem kept her from the ordinary convent and parish activity. I told a group of sisters that I would gladly bring Mary Jane the strength and love of God in Holy Communion. The nuns soon called me that she accepted the offer of daily, nourishing Communion, the Bread of Life. Being a reverent innovator, simply being "Father Sid," I began to sing aloud as I climbed the convent stairway that led to the second floor and Mary Jane's room. Three young and vivacious nuns accompanied me. They were surprised at me singing the appropriate church season song. They took it as an extra gift of honor to the personalized Holy Communion service for Mary Jane. They were immensely pleased as their joyous faces headlined their obvious feelings. I was singing a little off-key, yet with much heartfelt care: "O come, O come, Emmanuel, and ransom captive Israel."

When we entered the room I could tell Mary Jane was touched by my "Little Drummer Boy's" touch to this special sacrament. The five of us celebrated the love-filled Communion experience with meaningful, extemporaneous prayers of praise and thanks-giving. We concluded the holy event with a song sung by all of us: "They'll know we are Christians by our love, by our love. Yes, they'll know we are Christians by our love."

That special event, when I went the extra mile, began a friendship that blossomed into a very cherished one I enjoy to this day. She left immeasureable, positive markings on my deepest being.

13

A Real Family at Last!

To compound my work-a-holic problems, I
became a social activist, a real crusader of
humanitarian causes. I wanted to start a
revolution within the law-and-order-centered
church. I began different small groups. It
wasn't long until there were some very conservative Catholics that were calling me a
communist. Here I was simply forming small
groups of active Catholics according to
neighborhood blocks. We called them "little
parishes"—all belonging to the central parish
of St. Patrick's.

The ultra-conservative Catholics of St.
Patrick's looked upon such people-centered
activities as a danger to the Roman Catholic
Mother Church of basic monarchy, albeit a
sacred monarchy. Some of the conservative
thinking was that only they had what is right
and good for all Catholics. They looked upon
the little parishes where everyone had a voice
and advisory vote as too much like communist
cells. So, while some of us were trying to build
community in Christ, others were perceiving
the venture as communism creeping into the

Catholic Church. It may have been communist-looking in its small group approach, but not atheistic. These small groups were God- and Christ-centered.

For example, when Cesar Chavez was taking the cause of the migrant workers to the public and to the government leaders to demonstrate the plight and needs of the field workers, I wanted to be right there with him, marching with him, walking to Sacramento. Some of the small farmers that he was trying to awaken to the farm workers needs were in our parish. Farm parishioners said to me, "Father Sid, don't walk with Cesar Chavez. Please don't do that. You're going to step out in an area that will destroy your ministry."

I backed off and took to heart what they said and chose not to walk with Cesar. Ever since, I felt badly that I didn't stand with him and help.

During the little amount of time I took for myself, I tried studying various books and writings about the Scriptures, but never could quite muster up the venturing courage to get into the Scriptures alone.

At this time, during my San Jose ministry, I was also taking a look at my family situation and problems. I realized that my love had not gone out to my own family. Something blocked me from fully receiving and feeling Mom's saintly love until I was in my San Jose ministry—when I was almost forty years of age. I thank God I realized more fully and felt more deeply her total love for her children—for me—while she and I were still alive and could express that love.

Mom's kind of love expression involved the motto: "You don't touch. You have food and clothes and some fun things—that's all one needs. You do not need to touch." Nevertheless, I reached out. I reached out to touch personally and physically both Mom and Dad.

Along with my new awareness about Mother's special love for me, I began to realize that Dad needed me to love him, share with him and be concerned about him. I made special efforts to take him out regularly. I did take him to the minor and major seminaries in Mountain View and in Menlo Park. It was with deep joy and pride that I walked side by side with my Filipino dad at the seminaries and pointed out all the places of my priestly study and training—including all the spots where funny or crazy events took place.

I was astounded how many of his memories had much in common with my personal experiences during my eleven years of seminary life. While we walked together the halls and walking paths, a wonderful knitting of kindred spirits was initiated at those deeper, personal levels where only mutual respect and admiration abound. The love between father and son—long dormant for many complex human weaknesses—was germinating. There were blossomings in the sunshine and tears of our personal sharing.

As I was taking Dad and Mom to the homes of various friends and parishioners, at those friendly gatherings, I discovered how both my parents could bring life and laughter to people who accepted them and demonstrated their caring.

Mother shared simply and directly her childhood days, her six years of formal schooling, and her life as an Irish farm girl. I'm sure that those cows on the Burke farm listened and obeyed the unmistakable, commanding voice of that formidable Irish lass, my mother-to-be. She also told a number of personal stories of her upbringing and disciplining of me. Naturally, my friends enjoyed immensely "the secret, early disciplining" of such a restless maverick.

I loved her telling her stories. It was then I received an insight that I hope all children discover at sometime in life, even if it's in adult life, as it was in my case. Insight: Mother trained me as she herself was trained, as she thought was the only way to train. She was faithfully dedicated to "her troth." That insight freed me of so much misunderstanding and so many stored-up negative feelings. I was freed and could now love her more freely, not just honor and respect her by law.

At those same get-togethers, Dad was the "life of the party" with his ukulele. With his nimble fingers he played love songs and fun songs. He gave relevant comments between his song numbers, and ended each rendition with a fancy flare, flashing smile, and captivating eyes. His singing and playing were the entertainment highlights of those friendly socials. From this I also learned how much he loved his music. It was as if his music was another person that he loved so very much.

Once during a serious sharing experience with him, I asked him pointblank, "How did you make it through all those lonely times, the times we had you in the background and left you out of so much family activity?"

Without a moment's pause he replied, "I would go to my room and play my heart out, and I'd be all right. I knew I could always go on. I knew things would change. I knew things would be what they are today, my son."

How happy I was that there was a new relationship growing between my parents and me. My dreams were stretching. I deeply desired for them to enjoy each other more. I wanted to "spoil" them for the rest of their lives. Soon I was to be given a golden opportunity to do so. Their Fiftieth Wedding Anniversary was to take place on May 27 of that year, 1977.

Two special surprise events were planned for our "golden" parents. One was a quiet, beautiful celebration of a Mass in the Church of the Sacred Heart, the parish of our parents, and one in which I had my first ordination Mass.

Father Charles O'Conner, the pastor, rolled out the Irish green carpet for my family. He had an exquisitely-catered luncheon for our family and a few friends. This celebration had all the finest Irish touches and tastes included. It was handled as for a king and queen . . . in this case, a Filipino king and his queen. For an added treat, Mom told her stories and Dad sang his love and fun songs. When he sang "Meet Me Tonight In Dreamland," to his Margaret, there were only Irish eyes smiling amidst the tears.

It was a double joy for me to have them for a meal in my home parish—unlike my ordination dinner in 1954 when Dad "stayed" at home.

The second celebration took place in St. Patrick's parish. I picked up my parents early on Sunday morning in San Francisco and drove to San Jose for the surprise parish salute to their golden event. I presided over the Mass of Anniversary and Renewal. The music and words blended into a celebration of joyful love. I led them in a simple renewal of their wedding vows—for richer or poorer, in sickness and in health, etc. Typically, I improvised in order to make the meaning of the ceremony more personal to this special couple and to my parishioners. After the Communion time and before the dismissal prayer, I made time for the church to greet them personally. I stood near my parents in deepest exhilaration as the parishioners warmly greeted and praised my mother and father.

On this occasion, moments of joy were experienced when Mary Jane, Frank and Julie Barry approached, embraced and kissed my parents. For a Camelot moment I experienced the meaning of authentic family love, not just love according to common blood, but a deeper love by being a community united by a shared belief in Jesus Christ.

A few weeks later a special gift was offered

to my parents and me—a week's vacation in a home by the Pacific Ocean. Oh, did we have fun! We made meals together, walked in the cold ocean water. I dared to hold and hug more affectionately my mother and father. I knew that they loved it.

During one of the sharing times I stopped talking. We silently stood up and embraced and embraced lovingly for a long time. We embraced away all the past forty years of failings and complexities. Abundant tears assisted in the victorious washing and renewing of our spirits.

When we left our vacation spot, we sang most of the way home to San Francisco. Mom was singing in her Irish best. I, too, was singing, even exuberantly, still off-key. I hadn't sung with others in years. Dad, of course, was leading the singing and playing the ukulele— enjoying proudly and happily his new central role in a real family.

14

"Here's a Bible For You"

The end of my second year of ministry in San Jose was nearing. I was somewhat exhausted from my whirlwind approach to family, parish, and community needs and activities. I was more exhausted than I thought.

I'll take a breather real soon, I told myself daily, especially so after a single day of an overloaded schedule. Here one moment. Next moment over there. Back here now. Time for over there. People . . . people . . . people. Stop. Eat. Bed. Restless sleep. Up again. Here again. Dangerous living, certainly out of balanced control.

In the midst of all of this, an official letter arrived from the Archbishop of San Francisco. I couldn't believe the first few words: "You are hereby transferred . . ." I flung the letter across the room in anger and frustration. How can they do this to me? The harvest of community at St. Patrick's was only beginning. They were giving me only two years of generating Christian renewal. Usually they would give a priest five years in each parish assignment. Something was wrong. Somebody went after my scalp and got it. I stormed out of my rectory apartment and rushed toward the Sisters' convent.

Mary Jane quietly ushered me to one of the conference rooms, closed the door, and let me explode with a torrent of bitterness and resentment. I was certainly "out of control." Here was the priest known throughout the Bay Area as the smiling, sociable, dedicated worker, eccentric for sure, yet very accepted, even charming. My love-hungry heart in its new love of my parents, and people like Mary Jane, was now most vulnerable. The Archbishop's letter had triggered an eruption of that part of my heart that had suppressed and stored the anger and resentment for all those thirty-nine years of my "smiling" exterior.

"Mary Jane, I can't take it any more. I WON'T take it any more. They can't push me around like a piece of meat, a piece of property. This is the seventh move in only thirteen years. That's ridiculous. That's not human at all."

As my shooting-star outburst slowed to a simmering resentment, I could hear my quiet, faithful friend say, "Father Sid, why don't you phone the Archbishop and make an appointment to get some clarification for any questions you have?"

Her recommendation drew an immediate positive response: "Great idea. I'll do it right away."

With a twinkle in her eyes she said, "Why don't you walk in the yard for a while before you make that phone call?"

I caught her gentle message to walk off some of the heated anger before talking to the Archbishop. After my walk in the school yard, I phoned and talked to the Archbishop.

I asked if I could meet with him to discuss my being moved. I told him that I had to talk with him. I demanded to know WHY I was being changed, and if there was something wrong with my conduct. I was suspicious that the pastor, or some conservative group had asked to get me out of this parish. He looked at me and said, "No, Sid, it's not disciplinary action at all."

"I appreciate that."

"Quite frankly, the only reason we're moving you is there is a priest that is moving out of St. Vincent's, and we want to put you in there."

I had thought the reason I was being asked to leave was because of the sharing community that I had started, and because of hanging around the lay people and the nuns. It was such a beautiful time, and here I was being uprooted and moved from the people that I had learned to love.

At the farewell party Father Clem Johnson came to me with a pocket Bible. He commented, "Sid, here's a Bible for you. You're going to need it where you're going because from what I hear you are going to have a year of hell."

That jolting remark flashed in and out of my head as I gave my individual comments and hugs to all the parish friends. Near the end of the evening's events, I was called to the stage area of the auditorium. As I climbed the stairs I saw very clearly the brightly-painted sign that spread from one side of the stage to the other: IT IS GOOD FOR US TO BE HERE

TOGETHER. That was the expression with which I had begun most sermons or any other special community get-together.

I left the auditorium carrying Father Johnson's Bible (*Good News for Today*) and his friendly, though upsetting, comment to me: "You are going to need this Bible where you are going."

When I arrived at the new parish, I found that it was an intellectual one—one with many middle-class executives and professionals. As for the pastor, a preacher of renown, he wasn't exactly fire and brimstone, but he was close to it. There was much emphasis on the basic teaching of a very traditional catechism. Nothing much of Vatican Council renewal was in evidence—it certainly had more death to it than resurrection.

As the pastor showed me my room with a small desk in it, there was a cigarette burn on the desk. He said, "Look, Sid, that's what the last animal that lived in here did."

I knew inwardly that I was well on my way to burning out and having a breakdown or something, and his remark nearly sent me over the edge. Here I was trying to live in community where every man and woman is a brother or a sister and loved, and he's talking about a man as being an animal. As soon as I could, I excused myself from his guided tour and headed for the nearby beach for some urgently-needed fresh air.

As the days cut into weeks, I discovered I was becoming numb. I hugged but there was no feeling, no emotion. We shared in community but there was no more electricity. I was praying that I would get back to feeling but nothing happened. I was trying to love as a Christian should, yet I felt paralyzed. One day while sitting in my room I thought: *I need help. I need someone to get me out of this terrible depression.* I toyed with the idea of phoning Mary Jane, my faithful friend and confidant.

I hesitated out of embarrassment of mentioning that I needed psychiatric help. Thank God, I pushed the feeling aside and phoned her. After explaining the circumstances of my continuing exhausting anxiety, I told her I was considering a conference with a doctor, a psychiatrist. As was her custom, she was quiet for a few moments and then said, "Father Sid, that might be very beneficial. I want you to be in full health and strength as soon as possible. I'll be praying for you. Please let me know how the doctor's visit turns out."

"Thanks. I'll let you know. You can count on it."

That phone call turned the tide of my personal inner battle into a healthier direction. I knew there was a clinic where priests and nuns could go for psychiatric consultation. I decided to make a secret call. Slowly and deliberately my fingers dialed the number, and I made an appointment to an unknown psychiatrist at the other end. I was dead inside, but I wanted to get better. I wanted to live a normal, healthy life as a priest forever.

When I arrived at the clinic I was ushered into the room of a young doctor. He looked more like a young boy to me. He was an intern, but I decided that I was going to go all the way. I had to get help so I told him everything—my whole complicated life's story.

He suggested that group therapy would help, and prescribed some medication for immediate relief of my severe daily anxiety. I took the medication and went to the weekly group sessions. Since I was attending summer school, no one knew exactly what I was doing. I made my appointments so that I went from an early morning class to group therapy. By using this strategy, my pastor, Father Martin Thomas, thought I was at theology class all morning.

In the first session I mentioned I was a priest. Suddenly the social worker in charge of the group threw me a pornographic magazine and asked, "So, what do you think of this, Father?"

I flipped through the pages. I had no feeling or emotion except burning anger. I looked at him with glaring eyes and snapped, "Nothing!"

I continued the weekly sessions at the clinic, but my progress seemed deadly slow. I was beginning to talk about my sexual life and attitudes among the group, but also learned to listen and share others' feelings. Sometimes it concerned sex experiences that were almost unbelievable to me. My awareness of human conditions quickly and bluntly expanded in a very short time. It was clearly dawning on me that the other persons in my therapy group and I were greatly united in our humanness and in our hunger—even starvation—for real, lasting and fulfilling love. Our experiences differed greatly, yet all of us were struggling with a common and basic internal restlessness. We were living unsatisfying lives, even sexually. Those in the group who were hyperactive sexually were also unsatisfied, restless people. All of us had something missing in our lives or we wouldn't have been there weekly, in our searching condition.

After the group session, I would take a drive to the beach, walk a while in the invigorating ocean air, and then return to my pastoral duties at St. Vincent's.

One day I went to the refrigerator at the parish house to get a soft drink. The cook commented, "You have to buy your own soft drinks around here, Father."

That was my first encounter with anything as miserly as that in any parish. I had been warned by some priest friends that this pastor was going to be more than just a mere tightwad. Other indications of his stinginess in money matters dealt with the heating systems around the parish grounds. There was no heat in the hall when it was needed. There was no heat in the church when it was needed, not even for the 6:30 morning Mass. After some months of this craziness, I couldn't stand it any more. In a rage I ran into the rectory and shouted in the pastor's face: "Heat the church or say the Mass yourself." When the church continued to go unheated I took off for a few days, staying with some priest friends.

After I returned, I managed, with the help of some friends, to arrange a pleasant environment for the parishioners at their early, daily celebration of Mass. It was my secret.

One weekend my pastor called me "on the carpet" for not counting the collection during the Sunday morning Masses. "I want to meet the people as I ought, as one of their parish priests," I strongly told him.

He retorted, "I want you to count the collection with Father Joseph on Sunday mornings. Period!"

A bitter verbal exchange was avoided at that time either because it was Sunday, or maybe my group sessions were proving beneficial. They had demonstrated to me the importance of expressing rather than repressing my answer, but in various, constructive ways. So I walked away. In fact, I walked right out the front door in order to meet the people in front of the church after the Masses. Later I went to the parish workroom and counted the collection with Father Joseph. Father Thomas wanted no one to count the parish money except the priests. Money seemed to be all that my pastor thought about.

I consider that one long year of my life in that rectory as a life surrounded by darkness. It was like living in one of those eerie mansions of an English horror novel. The pastor appeared to be a man of coldness and darkness, especially in his aloof attitude toward people and their ordinary needs.

The pastor and I continuously battled verbally, or in silence. The weekly skirmishes took their toll on my active, though strained, constitution. Unfortunately, I had abandoned the group therapy sessions after only three months. The group nurse phoned and encouraged me to continue—for my personal benefit. I said, "No, thank you, nurse." It was a bad decision. I had unknowingly refused the life-preserver of the weekly group sessions during my storm-tossed ministry at St. Vincent's.

One afternoon at three, I was called to the rectory conference room. A young gentleman had asked for me. During the personal conference he revealed a series of adultery experiences. He was in his twenties, apparently an executive from his appearance and speaking manner. He expressed his deep guilt feelings over his weakness. He spoke quickly and gave all his comments in a few short minutes. When I was about to say something to him, he jumped from his chair and yelled, "Surprise, Sid! I'm Eddie Garvey, the new priest in the neighboring parish."

I, too, jumped from my chair and yelled something earthy as we embraced and laughed and laughed. I had heard about the new type of priests being trained: self-confident, extremely bright, innovators, etc. This young cleric was all of that and more. His wit, humor and sense of craziness were infectious. We became friends quickly.

Soon Eddie and I began a prayer group for priests. We met in a different parish each Saturday after the evening's confessional services. Ten of us met and prayed regularly. After the hour prayer time, we socialized for another hour over coffee and dessert.

The unbelievable happened. The ten of us

were in my parish church one night after 9:00 P.M. We were reading quietly before sharing our thoughts. All of us were wearing relaxing clothes, short-sleeved shirts and jackets, as was our custom for the prayer sessions. Suddenly my pastor strides up the center aisle, muttering aloud for all to hear: "It's after nine o'clock, Father Custodio, time to turn off the lights and close the church."

He saw only the back of our heads as he walked by us and then into the room behind the altar area. He then clicked off the lights. Obviously, Father Thomas didn't recognize a well-liked, young Monsignor Jim Fahey, or he wouldn't have turned off the lights and left us sitting in the dark. Had all of the men there been laymen Christians, the action of my pastor would still have been equally unbelievable for it was un-Christian action. The young Monsignor in our group quieted our anger by a promise to write my pastor a letter of fraternal displeasure.

From the turning out of the lights event, a series of events took place with regularity, events that would lead to my liberation from St. Vincent's. The most serious episode between us occurred on a Saturday night. I found my Sunday schedule thrown on the floor of my room. It was almost midnight. The priest house was silent and dark—but not for long. I ran down the hallway to my pastor's suite. I pounded on his door shouting, "Come out of there you ..." In utter rage I continued slamming his door with my fist: "Come on out and fight!"

Thank God, my pastor stayed in his locked room that night. There was certainly enough tragedy in that house without me adding another load to it from a tornado of uncontrollable rage. Soon after that incident I dropped into depression again. Once more I was filled with anxiety and a very shaky physical system. It was a strange and terrifying experience to be constantly haunted by negative attacks: "You can't make it, Father Sid. Look at your hands, they are trembling. You are going to lose everything. No hope for you now, Father Sid."

I refused to eat meals with my pastor. Consequently, almost every night I would go to hamburger places or coffee shops. Often I wouldn't eat a regular meal. I'd nibble on candy and other sweets throughout the day. Nutritionally, I was harming myself seriously. Nevertheless, I continued my over-active ministry in my parish responsibilities, and also in priestly work throughout the city of San Francisco. Many times I would go many miles to help someone. I was happy any time I could get away from the rectory of St. Vincent's.

This type of struggle between my pastor and me could not continue. Parishioners were talking about the situation, and were taking sides. Finally, the pastor had had it. He went to the Archbishop and requested that I be transferred as soon as possible. Shortly I was notified that I was being sent to St. Peter's Parish in Pacifica.

A number of parishioners reacted strongly, and in my favor. The group was led by one of the couples in the "marriage enrichment" program, Ed and Helen Moore. Ed wrote the words of the petition and circulated it with the help of other couples. After all the signatures were gathered they were brought by Ed and a few others to the Archbishop.

Naturally, I heard about this action. It meant a great deal to me that some lay people were not going to take my removal in silent surrender. Ed put a copy of the petition in my rectory mailbox. I could only read the first few lines before giving way to a flood of tears—tears of victory after a bloody battle. I shall always remember the words from the first paragraph of that layman document: "Your Excellency, we want you to realize that our priest, Father Sid Custodio, has brought Jesus Christ into our lives."

At the end of my farewell Mass I looked at the parishioners with much love as I raised my right hand for the special, concluding blessing. After the blessing Ed Moore and a friend, Reece Jansen, stood up at the front of the congregation. With great feeling Ed asked, "May we dedicate this final song of the Mass to Father Sid for his priestly service to the people of St. Vincent's?" Ed and Reece then led the congregation in the hymn: "Now thank we all our God for all His gifts and blessings."

If the two-year ministry at St. Patrick's in San Jose was my "Camelot," the year at St. Vincent's was my miniature, emotional "War and Peace." I wondered what my new assignment in Pacifica would be like. The pastor was a man I knew only by name.

15

"God, Why Have You Deserted Me?"

When I arrived at St. Peter's, I rang the doorbell, knowing that Bob Duryea would answer it. He opened the door and said, "Welcome, Sid," and then hugged me. That was a shock to my emotional system after my past year. We then chatted a while.

"Sid," he said, I know you're into theology, and I know you are trying to find answers. I'd like to show you this letter from the Archbishop."

It read:

> *Dear Father Bob,*
>
> *Your new assistant is going to be Sid Custodio. As you probably know, he is loved by many people, but at this time in his life he needs much direction. Yes, he needs to really watch his timetable. He is liable to do a lot, but give him heavy direction.*
>
> *Sincerely yours,*

After reading the letter he looked at me and asked, "Sid, how shall we work this out? What shall we do? How would you like to arrange the Masses, etc.?"

I could not believe what I was hearing from the mouth of this tall, gentle-voiced pastor. He was talking to me—person to person—co-pastor to co-pastor. He was saying that we were a pastoral team, a family, and in a real sense, brother Christians. His manner, his voice, his whole being seemed to reflect the new Biblical theology of Vatican Council II. I kept wiggling my toes to prove I was really listening to a Catholic pastor talking in this personal and Biblical way to me, an assistant. No, I wasn't in heaven yet. However, in respect to a parish rectory environment I was in clerical heaven. I loved it and tried to relax in his company. He requested that I call him by his first name only.

There was a deep feeling bothering me as I left Bob to get used to my new apartment in the back of the rambling, ranch-style rectory: *You might be in a heavenly parish, Father Sid. Too bad you have exhausted yourself to the point of no return—emotionally, mentally, physically and spiritually. Too bad, Father Sid. It's too late now to enjoy your new heaven.*

Most of the members of the oceanside parish were young and ordinary working people with an openness and enthusiasm. It was such joy to be with them and work and grow together.

It was only a few days when Bob said, "Sid, I'm leaving for vacation. Take over. We don't have a housekeeper. We have a secretary, and she'll cook the evening meal before she leaves in the afternoon."

At the time I didn't know it but Bob had a

very special reason for not having any housekeeper live in the rectory. He and I were the only residents—it was ours alone.

Bob had just left when there was a riot at the shopping center. When the police arrived, some were ready to mace the kids. Instead of macing one of the kids, one policeman maced himself. The riot event made the headlines, and the seaside city of Pacifica was upset and buzzing. The kids were upset but wanted to talk. I said, "If they'd like to talk it over, they can come to St. Peter's." I thought Bob wouldn't mind. Within an hour and a half the kids were there—boys, girls, and men and women. Some were "high."

I asked if I could sit in and listen to what was going on.

"Sure, Father."

Then one militant stood up saying, "Let's burn down the shopping center. They beat us up. Let's burn it to the ground."

This type of talking went on for a while. Finally, I asked, "May I speak?"

"Yeah."

"Hey, I know the mayor." (I had just heard about him.) "Why don't I phone and ask him to come and talk with us?"

"Yeah, that's good, Father."

The mayor came and they argued back and forth. They gave him their twelve demands and he left.

Then big mouth Sid said, "I'll get you a lawyer; he'll help you with a plan of action."

The lawyer came and showed them how to

go through an effective process of airing grievances. We had a town meeting, complete with television. Father Sid, the bold, gave the talk of welcome and hope.

In the meantime the mayor had read the twelve demands and got defensive.

Some adults stood up and blasted the kids. Wiser adults won the evening by respecting the way the youth presented their needs to the city assembly. In the end the city agreed to furnish more recreation space for the youth—space that was badly needed. It was a real victory for youth and adults.

I had decided to give a series of lectures on the Mass, and the role of Jesus Christ in the Mass. I was going everywhere giving out cards, inviting people to come. They were lined up like the Super Bowl, men and women in their twenties and thirties. They were hungry to know the risen Christ of the Mass. In my wildest imaginations I never thought so many would come. I had become popular because I helped the kids. "This guy's human," said one. "He touched me," said another. "He hugs I hear," said another. "He's for the people of the parish. His head isn't so high up in the clouds that he doesn't hear. He can relate to us."

When Bob returned from vacation and heard all that was going on he seemed to be quite excited and said, "Sid, I know you and many of the men of the parish have been sharing somewhat. I want you to sit down for I have something I want to share with you that I've never shared. Sid, I'm married, and have been for five years. I have a son, Paul. I named him after Pope Paul."

His candid revelation struck like a bombshell. I could have screamed—someone had really opened himself to me! My joyous response was a big hug. "Bob, thank you for sharing with me. This is the first time in my forty years that any priest has opened up his problems to me, inviting me into his life."

He went to the phone, called his wife, and had me talk to her. We made arrangements to get together. Even though his being married was such an extreme situation outside of the most serious church law, I was inwardly at peace about it. I was also thrilled that he was so honest with me. I was genuinely happy that a priest was happily married and was ministering so effectively.

We made an excellent team as co-pastors. We had been blessed with different talents and gifts which complemented each other. Our spiritual teamwork produced an abundant harvest for Jesus Christ. Thanks to this married priest's openness, encouragement and renewed theology, I was blessed with the freedom to reach out to all adults and youth to form sharing groups centered in the power and love of Jesus Christ. Thanks to our unique leader, married and dedicated, St. Peter's parish was committed to personal Christian growth and community service.

The adult groups that I directed soon blossomed into even closer bonds as caring Christians who reached out to serve. At the celebrations of Mass on weekdays and

Sundays the presence of a loving God was poured upon us. When those Christians vigorously sang, "They'll know we are Christians by our love," I knew that they shared that genuine love throughout the following week.

I was so happy with seeing the harvest of adults and teens. They were Christian and growing more and more. It was heaven on earth. Yet my emotional and mental condition was getting progressively worse. I was extremely nervous. I was driving myself on an empty physical and mental tank.

Bob and I drove to Los Gatos for the Christmas Eve dinner with his wife, Lu, and son Paul. It was a different family experience for me, especially hugging the wife of my pastor. Then we rushed back for the midnight Mass, which is one of the major events of the year. I caught a cold running around in the night air and could not seem to shake it. I felt weak.

Now I was often going to doctors who diagnosed various illnesses, yet discovered no causes. My throat was hurting constantly. I had to cut back to a very limited activity. I was still saying Mass on Sunday, even though it was very difficult for me to get through it. I left the church quickly afterwards to lie down in bed because I would be perspiring yet shaking with chills.

Somehow God gave me the spirit and energy for two major events that occurred suddenly—one tragic and the other jubilant. There was a push-and-shove fight at the local public high school between two youngsters at lunchtime. This led to an afternoon scuffle in which one boy used a knife that penetrated the back of the other, ending up in cutting his lung. The injured boy, one of my parishioners from the youth program, was dead that evening. The tragedy rocked the community.

I went to visit the parents of the victim. The father was enraged and had all the human urges of going over to the other boy's home to batter him to a pulp. I listened, and was moved to unleash all the love left in my spirit. After many hours, we prayed together and agreed to meet at Mass the next morning.

Morning weekday Mass was celebrated in the front portion of the rectory. That morning a number of teens participated, along with the victim's parents. We continued doing this each morning before the funeral date. We listened daily to Jesus Christ speaking to us through His Scripture Word about life and death, about anger and forgiveness. I saw the miracle change in the father of the slain boy. As he listened deeply to the words of life in the Mass he soon demonstrated a truly marvelous forgiving spirit to the young boy who had done the ugly deed.

The other major event was jubilant. Two of my teen group entered the folk music contest of the Bay Area Catholic Youth Organization. It was a personal thrill to direct and manage them. These two young talents proceeded to win the first prize awards. As an extra prize, they were asked to perform later in the month at a major archdiocesan banquet. This was the opening of a fine spiritual and recreational center for youth in the lovely Russian River area. I drove the music duo the sixty miles to the event.

While at this affair, I realized something was seriously wrong. I felt that I was about to drop dead and disintegrate. I asked the center's director for a quiet place for me to take a rest. I stayed in bed the whole day, feeling frozen in spirit as well as body. I was out of the tranquilizer pills that used to help me "get by." The week earlier I had urged a doctor for a refill prescription. He gently refused saying, "Father Sid, I've done this for you for a long time now. I can't do any more unless you come in to see me." He was doing the wise refusal, since I hadn't seen him in nearly two years.

Even without the survival benefit of any pills, I struggled to get to the end of the banquet to hear "my" kids play and sing before the large assembly of people, including the Archbishop himself. I managed a smile, as usual, when the Archbishop walked by and said, "Fine work, Father Sid."

Somehow I drove home safely that night. Shortly thereafter I fell apart internally. I was doing things that attracted attention and upset numerous people. I would celebrate the various sacraments—Masses, marriages, baptisms, etc.—in any way I chose. I'd always do the basic or essential words and actions, but would innovate and create spontaneous activities that would mean much to me personally. Those worship innovations that violated the prescribed forms and structure of the Catholic Church traditions upset many people. My closer parish friends knew from my strange behavior in church and around the parish, that something unhealthy was happening to me.

One time a visiting priest was so shaken by what I was doing during some marriage ceremony that he got up and stormed out. I was doing so many strange things and didn't know why. One Sunday morning while in the kitchen fixing breakfast, a voice spoke to me saying, "You can't say Mass. You don't like saying the words exactly as they are. In good conscience, Sid, you can't follow the church's ceremonies."

At that I packed my things into my little Volkswagen and took off. Before I left I told the priest that I couldn't say Mass any more as the church required it. I had to be myself, and in that state of mind I left. I headed for San Jose instinctively, and arrived at my former parish, St. Patrick's.

The parish was holding its annual church fiesta with games, food and other social activities. I was half in the real world and half in an unreal world. In the unreal world, I considered myself as an ambassador of brotherhood and peace. I was dressed in black slacks and a heavy-knit green turtleneck sweater—my trademark in the unsettling sixties.

At the amusement rides I noticed a white man who was in charge of the rides treating his black helper in a very discourteous manner. His calling him "boy" drew my attention. I marched right up to that hefty boss saying,

"Sir, don't speak to your assistant like that. He's another beautiful human being as you and I are." Instead of taking a poke at me, especially since I wasn't in my priestly garb, he mumbled, "No problem, I didn't mean anything anyway."

A St. Patrick's parishioner handed me a drink. "Here, Father, enjoy a drink on me."

"Peace, brother," I replied weirdly. When the man turned to leave, I dumped the drink into a nearby trash can. However, my benefactor noticed my action and shouted at me, "What in the blazes did you do that for? You accepted the drink. You say, 'Peace, brother,' and then you throw the drink away."

Living only partly in reality, I uttered, "Don't worry about it, brother. I just don't drink. Besides, one day I'll be saving the whole world." Obviously I had flipped out. The man stared at me for a moment in silence then moved away in a hurry.

Though I was in this unstable condition, none of the priests commented on it. They welcomed me into the rectory. The pastor generously stated, "Sid, you can stay here as long as you want. Hope you get things straightened out with Pacifica Parish. They respect and need you."

After a few days I made a phone call to Father Frank Carlton, my friend from San Mateo days. I told him I needed some rest badly. I asked if he could break away on emergency leave for a few days and take me to some retreat place in the nearby Santa Cruz Mountains. He said he'd check it out immediately. In less than ten minutes he phoned back. "Everything is okay here. I can pick you up in thirty minutes." I thanked him, prepared a few clothes, and waited outside the rectory.

On our way to the mountain retreat we stopped at an observation parking area. For a few minutes we looked over parts of the panoramic Santa Clara Valley. I began singing a few lines of the song, "On a clear day, I can see forever . . ." then said, "Someday I'm going to save all that I can see."

An hour later, Frank and I were settled by a fireplace in a cozy bungalow retreat—ready to unwind. I was so jittery and confused that I went for a walk alone. When I returned in an hour, another priest had arrived. When he saw me he said, "Sid, Joan Baez is in Santa Cruz to talk to the priests of the area. How about going over to see her?"

"Sure, let's go," I answered as I jerked at several strands of colored beads that were used as room dividers in the bungalow and wrapped the beads around my neck.

When we arrived Joan was already speaking. During the question and answer period I piped up, questioning, "Hey, you're making all this money talking peace and anti-establishment, yet you are making money off the establishment."

There was dead silence for a while.

After the Baez seminar, Frank and Ray hustled me outside into the car. As we headed for our hide-away, I began singing opera songs.

This was really strange since I didn't know any opera songs.

When the three of us were sitting comfortably near the crackling fire, suddenly I got up and approached the fireplace, kneeling by the side of it. I took out my wallet and was tearing up the paper money pieces one by one—a few fives, a ten, and a twenty. After I tore up each one I threw it into the fire. My priest companions were silent and stunned. As I continued my bizarre behavior, they came and pulled me away from the fire.

"Sid, what are you doing that foolishness for? Don't do it!"

I proclaimed, "Money is worth nothing when you have something more precious in your life."

There was much uneasiness in the house that night as we headed for our rooms and some sleep. "Sid, you take it easy and get some rest," Frank counseled as we walked down the narrow hallway.

The next morning Frank invited us to go for a swim at the home of one of his friends in nearby Los Gatos. I couldn't swim in deep water, but I agreed to go. We met several other priests there. I didn't know that Frank had arranged for a priest psychologist to be among the group at the pool. Frank knew I needed to be checked out immediately.

Something happened at the pool that frightened everyone—especially me. Eddie Matthews, a young priest, who didn't know me well or my swimming ability, pushed me into the water, thinking it was shallow. I called, "Be careful, Ed, remember I can't swim." However, a few minutes later I stood at the very edge of the deep end of the pool, looking down into the water. I saw something like a jewel at the bottom. Something inside me urged me to "Jump in!" I did. Instantly I realized I was out of breath and drowning. I sensed I was dying. As I was about to burst from lack of air, I said, "Here I am, Lord. I'm yours." The next thing I remembered was someone grabbing my hair and pulling me to the side of the pool. They were shoving on my back, and soon I began coughing. One of the priests said, "Look, he's coughing up milk like a little baby."

That night at dinner the psychologist Frank had called and I got into a big fight. He said, "You know, Sid, you think you're the Messiah and you have a Messiah complex."

During this heated discussion, Frank went into another room and phoned the Archbishop. When he returned he said, "Sid, you are wanted on the phone."

The Archbishop, in a very somber and yet authoritative way, said, "Sid, I want you to follow Father Frank's directions explicitly and go to the hospital tonight. Will you promise me that?"

"Sure, Your Excellency. I'll do exactly as you request."

That night Frank took me to a nearby hospital. I was put through a series of psychiatric tests. They gave me a bunch of riddles. I answered each one like a wise guru. I don't know if I gave them the correct answer or not, but I had an answer for everything. After all, I was the Messiah and I knew everything. I was admitted for a seventy-two-hour observation period, but was there for eight weeks—eight unforgettable weeks! There were other priests in the psychiatric ward also.

I was given tranquilizers that put me to sleep. I thought I slept twenty hours out of every twenty-four-hour day. After three weeks I developed hives all over my body, and my mouth turned to cotton. The senior doctor seemed to be shocked and yelled at one of the interns, "What do you have him on THAT for? Take him off of that medication immediately."

When I came off of it, I was on a "high." Then I went from the Messiah complex to thinking I was going to be the next pope. It was all so vivid in my mind, even in its unreality. I chose a name. I would be called Pope Joseph. A week later I thought I was God the Father and would go around the ward ministering to all the sick people.

My final days on the ward were filled with a low, sick feeling. I was back to reality. I found the reality of being me—Sid in a hospital and wanting to be alone. It was a heavy experience. I didn't want anyone to know what happened to me. I didn't want to see anyone I knew—no one . . . no one!

God arranged a ray of sunshine and hope for me every day through a nurse. During personal conferences, Phyllis would say, "Father Sid, things will change. You will get better. You will get better."

That was the song of hope my spirit

needed. I clung to her words and in my darkest moments I would say them aloud.

Besides Phyllis and her touching encouragement, my faithful brother Ed came every night after dinner. Usually, I was quiet all those evenings. Nevertheless, playing cards with a brother who loved me filled me with a desire to keep going, to survive, to get well. Ed has always been the equivalent of the entire Notre Dame University rooting section for me in many daring adventures.

Why? I would scream to myself in my hidden thoughts, *have I ended up with no more heart, no more spirit? Didn't I give everyone a piece or chunk of my heart to help or to be a friend in their need?* I guess I was saying what Jesus said on His cross: "My God, my God, why have You deserted me?"—I added: "and in a psychiatirc ward?"

The big moment of hospital release came in July. It was a narrow victory for me. In meeting with my psychiatrist—a young, talented resident doctor—it appeared the doctor was not going to approve my release. Actually, he didn't know my situation very well since he had a number of patients under his care. He had been my assigned physician only a few weeks. He was hesitant to make such a big decision. Phyllis stepped into the stumbling conference. "He's near the goal line, doctor. Let him score," she said.

The doctors always needed the valuable input of the ward nurses, since they were with us daily and knew us best. My doctor readily took Phyllis' recommendation and signed the official paper of release. After he left the room she smiled. I hugged her with the biggest "Thank you" embrace that was in me. In five minutes I packed and left the hospital.

Where was I to go?

Father Clem Johnson, who had given me the pocket Bible gift, invited me to stay at his San Francisco parish of St. Mark's. His pastor had approved my recuperating there. I was thrilled. The enthusiasm of the new adventure helped greatly.

Family reunion, 1953
Mom, sister-in-law Kay, Dad
Ed, Jim, Sid (front).

16

The Missing Link

After a few days at St. Mark's, I realized I was still unbelievably weak in body and spirit. My pastoral duties were minimal, almost nothing, at first. Mainly, I was available only if the other priests were occupied with other tasks. On one occasion, I walked to the conference room in the front of the rectory and met a middle-aged man. He was well-dressed and in a professional level of work.

He began his story of experiences as a homosexual. He was filled with anxiety and guilt. I listened with deep care, as was my custom over the fifteen years of ministry. As any counselor knows, intensive listening is energy demanding. In less than fifteen minutes my mental tank was on "empty." Inwardly, I was yelling: "Stop it, please! Please, stop it! I can't listen any more. I have nothing for you, sir."

Externally, I gave the troubled man my eyes of compassion and my empathy. I'm sure he caught my understanding and acceptance of him as a hurting individual, for I, too, was suffering so much personally. I told him I would arrange a brief series of sessions for him with a professional counselor—if he chose to travel that course of action. He agreed. I phoned a respected counseling service that offered free community services, checked out some names of counselors and gave them to him.

"It's up to you now, Jim. Follow through with your decision. I'm rooting for you. I'd like to hear from you how things go."

Jim left the rectory, obviously more relieved, even hopeful. I went upstairs and flopped on the bed, fatigued and sweating.

At my first public worship service I stood by "Big Clem" Johnson and presented the bread of life, Holy Communion, to my parishioners. A very simple action ordinarily. That day it was major and a breakthrough for me, even a triumph. I felt so good about it that I actually imagined myself as tall and big as Big Clem, all six feet and five inches of him. I'm some inches shorter, but not that day. His encouraging presence next to me made a big difference. He didn't show tears of joy on that occasion—he usually doesn't—but I saw the equivalent of them on his happy Irish face and in those smiling Irish eyes. Father Sid, the "baby" priest, took his first step that day in his return to public ministry.

I was to officiate at a wedding. It was terrifying because I had the dry heaves often since leaving the hospital. Before the wedding there was an ever-constant thought: Would I get through it or get sick? As it came time to perform the ceremony I chickened out and phoned a newly-ordained neighboring priest.

While he performed the wedding, I sat in my room again going through emptiness . . . real emptiness. I had a rock-bottom feeling in me. It was a failure, a single failure. But in my mental state I considered it total inadequacy for ministry.

Ed and Helen, of my St. Vincent's days, were my salvation. Every Saturday I would go there for dinner and regain enough composure to continue. Thanks to Ed and Helen and the Irish caring nuns, I was finding my way back into a life of reality and effective ministry. Big Clem was an enormous encourager. Ed and Helen invited me to have dinner with them my first Easter at the parish. Dad was eighty-five at the time, and came, but Mother couldn't make it.

Dad, with his song-filled spirit, captured all their hearts and attention. I overheard one person say, "The father is more alive than the son." I couldn't bear this. I looked at Dad and truly he was socially appealing, fully blossomed. Here I was at forty-one fully frightened. Yes, I was as frightened as any little child could be. I was only a shell of a man—that was all that was left of me.

As I left that unforgettable Easter dinner, I told my much-loved friend Ed, "I can't make it any more as a parish priest. In fact, I don't think I can take anything anymore. I'm going to commit myself again into the hospital."

He stopped me in my tracks by pulling me aside into a room off the hallway. "Father Sid, you can make it. I know you can. Don't go back in there, please! Promise you'll try another week first. Promise me at least that. We love you."

The Christian community of the sisters, the priests, and the parishioners enlivened my spirit to the point of HOPING again, dreaming again, setting targets again.

Then it happened suddenly. Unexpectedly. Wonderfully. I met a lovely lady who captured my total attention. She not only made me sing to myself "The Impossible Dream," but this poised, intelligent lady of dignity made me start dreaming the impossible: an intimate, life-long friendship. Together we could be happier and more effective from the relationship. That was a great dream indeed. For me, as a priest, however, it definitely was more on the impossible side of real life.

Seminars were being held for junior high teachers to learn the latest audio-visual methods of instruction. Three hundred were to be in attendance in the city of San Francisco . . . that was the predicted estimate. Only eight showed up. There were two nuns in attendance, and one was Audrey. There were to be three sessions. I prided myself on being able to remember everyone's name. At the second session I quoted everyone's name, but when I looked at her I went blank.

Quickly she commented, "How come you don't remember my name?"

"I don't know, but I would like to," I said.

Quietly she said, "I'm Sister Audrey."

At that I glibly said, "Real pleasure meeting you again. Next week I will remember your name." At the time I didn't realize it, but

Audrey remembered me from my summer school days when I'd gather all the nuns and priests to enjoy fellowship and song. She kept her distance from me at that time because she was afraid of too much of this community love business. She had also heard that I was one of the big ringleaders. Many had warned her, "Stay away from that guy—he's a very love-hungry man."

As the weeks progressed I was feeling much better. I was gaining back my assurance and confidence. I received a call from a school asking if I would come and give a talk. I accepted. I taught the children on preparation for Confirmation. My subject was: "How to be a young Christian adult"—Cursillo style. After I finished, the teacher, Audrey, came and said hello. We were semi-friendly for a few minutes, and I left. It wasn't long until I received another phone call from the same convent asking if I would give a talk to the nuns on a retreat, and say Mass. I was delighted and answered, "Yes!"

I went to the convent and only Audrey came out. The rest were in other cars so there were Audrey and I in my car alone. She had on black stockings and a new dress, no habit. Her group of nuns dressed in regular clothes at that time. I drove her to the retreat and loved every minute of it.

When we arrived, the morning conference was already in session. I was scheduled to say the afternoon Mass and give my talk. I was feeling lively, but still required a lot of rest, so when we arrived I went to a room and rested for two hours. I then said Mass for all the sisters. I felt I had much to say that was uplifting and gave some good news that called us to respond with a total commitment of love. After the retreat I invited Sister Audrey to return to the city with me. She readily approved. I loved it. It was a touch of heaven to me.

The next morning I woke up and phoned Audrey's convent, but as soon as the phone started ringing I hung up. I dialed the number again—and hung up! I was rationalizing to myself: *Sid, you make so many friends and then to some extent you desert them.* I paused, sat for a while, prayed for some time. I knew this situation was different. I didn't know it, but it was daring for someone like me to do this. I was recently recovered from a breakdown, but inside something said, "Yes." I was peaceful.

Then I dialed the number again and Audrey answered. Eagerly I asked, "Sister Audrey, would you like to take a walk on the beach or something?"

She simply said, "Yes."

I felt like Snoopy at supper time. I was ecstatic. I picked her up and took her to a church fiesta. Here I was, a priest, taking an unchaperoned nun to a church gathering. We were like little children. We played every game there. We were innocent, naive, and very indiscreet. We then went to the beach and walked for what seemed hours. As we were returning to the parking lot I held her hand to help her get up the hill. When we got to the top

I didn't let her hand go nor did she pull it away.

Suddenly I realized that I was going to be late for a birthday party for the pastor. "Forgive me, Audrey, but I've got to get you back quick. I'm late already for the pastor's birthday party. I'll phone you later tonight, okay?"

She nodded "Yes."

When I arrived at the parish I was reprimanded and very embarrassed. However, the joy inside outweighed the rest of the feelings.

For the next year and a half Audrey and I were meeting lots and lots of times. We'd go for an ice cream or a ride or a walk on the beach. Every time we met we would have a prayer session before we began our outing. Deep inside I knew this lovable lady wasn't merely a wild and wonderful infatuation.

I began showing her picture to my friends, but soon I became so deeply in love with her that I was experiencing occasional attacks of fear about where our wonderful love was leading us. We definitely were both swimming in the ocean-deep waters of sharing and touching intimacy.

The first time Audrey and I went to a restaurant together was soon after our enjoyable walk on the beach. The restaurant was very near my parish, and not far from the school where she was the principal. We were in no way meeting secretly. We merely wanted to be good friends who cared and shared, even honorably as the celibate people that we were. I recall the first dinner because of Audrey's honesty and directness. At this time of renewed Christian customs, people in religious life called each other by their first names in the spirit of friendship.

"Sid," said Audrey, "I've heard and know you have many friends, both men and women. I've heard much about you among my sisters who went to summer school classes with you. I'm glad you have many friends. But I want to get one thing settled. Sid, I'm either number one or I don't want to enter a close friendship."

That was not an easy statement to swallow while one is only starting his dinner salad. Here it was my special night out with Miss Fascination, my lady of beauty, and reserve—and here I was getting bombshell statements.

In the course of the three-hour restaurant experience, I shared peacefully and honestly my entire odyssey of relationships from the eighth grade to that moment. I also shared the breakdown and burnout episode three years earlier. To my supreme joy, Audrey answered warmly and openly, "I thank you, Sid, for sharing yourself so fully. I hope to share more of me and my life with you also. That is not an easy thing for me to do. Basically, I trust only my mother, father and family. I do not allow anyone else, only God, to get real close to me. I like you and I don't even know why. You are almost everything opposite of me and of my kind of friend. You are so social, so extroverted, so public, so affectionate even in public. Usually, I don't like any of those qualities in my friends. Yet, I like you. But I have to know right away—am I going to be number one or not?"

During the dessert and coffee, I said, "I'm beginning a daring and dangerous relationship with you. I have many friends and families who love and embrace me in genuine care. Still I'm moved to reach out and begin something very special—even after a total burnout that crippled me greatly for over two years. If you can accept me as I am, I can honestly give you my commitment to your friendship as my number one priority. Remember, I want to be single always and remain a celibate minister—that's my only goal—an intimately sharing companion who has the same ideal."

Audrey accepted my sincere offer and commitment to her with a quiet, smiling joy. She is not highly demonstrative, but her eyes tell it all. Her eyes were eager and dancing.

We left that Daly City restaurant with the impossible dream shared by us both. In a few minutes we reached her residence. I pulled over to the curb near her front door. I leaned over toward her, put my right arm around her shoulder and drew her toward me. "Audrey, thanks for a very special evening. I'll phone you tomorrow." I kissed her on the cheek tenderly and quickly. She was not the hug-and-kiss type. Then she kissed me on the cheek in return, which was an unexpected surprise and bonus. Even though I had a number of loving friends who dearly care for me and show it, this simple affection on Audrey's part generated a brand new spirit deep within me.

As she got out of my car, she turned to me

and said, "Sid, I know you write poetry. Would you write one for me about yourself?"

"Sure, Audrey. Good night."

Driving home was a happy experience because of feeling so alive. I started composing the poem I promised.

The next day I put the poem on paper and dropped it off at Audrey's school office. I didn't get to see her that day, however. In the lines of poetry that flowed from me I wanted to tell Audrey my inner feelings and behavior patterns:

A Cater-fly

Like a crawling caterpillar,
I'm scarcely alive at times—
With little listening to all.

When it comes to speaking,
I plod slowly, slowly along
Often with stopping or silence.

Yet there are moments when I fly
With a joy that begets joy—
Bringing forth self-worth from
many.

Frequently I am seen
As sharing courage and dreams—
Like a new, risen butterfly.

With so many persons now asking
themselves: Who am I?
I find myself to be a constant
changing cater-fly.

P.S.: Here I am, Audrey. Hope you
still like me.

Audrey enjoyed the poetry and said, "Sid,
you're my number one. I want you to know
that. I've never said that to anyone—only to
my family."

Needless to say, that self-revelation from
Audrey, my quiet princess, made the buried
"love song" part of me rise to the fore again. I
knew I'd find a song someday that described
Audrey and me.

Three months later, Audrey and I parked
by her home after another delightful marathon
dinner together. Something was bothering me
so I blurted out, "Audrey, I'm worried about
our relationship. I love the sharing and I need
it a lot, but I share about 90% of the time and
you share only 10%. I need someone, a best
friend, who shares her needs, strengths and
weaknesses, her honest motives, goals and
dreams. I'm aware that a person doesn't just
sit down and spill out all that like a computer. I
know it's a gradual process for most people.
But I don't get any indications of our relationship growing mutually in that area. I want a
friend who will share like that. It means the
friend would be presenting herself to me fully
and trustingly. I can't continue our relationship without mutual, trusting sharing, even
though I like you a lot."

Five or ten minutes of silence followed.

"Sid, that's the hardest thing on earth for
me to do—to talk about myself to anyone and

about the things inside me. I live by the motto: 'Trust and talk personally only to your family.' That's how I've been all my life. I want to continue our friendship. I will share whatever you ask because I trust and respect you a great deal.''

The balanced mutual sharing became a part of our every outing, at least during the excursions we included time for lengthy conversation. The relationship grew, and some fear clouds grew along with it.

I decided to have a counseling conference with a respected, and well-known Carmelite priest who every other year lived the hermit's life of solitude, bare necessities, and communion with Almighty God. I intended to bring up three questions of major importance to me: Is it possible to have a close woman friend and still be a Catholic priest? How can I develop and become a man of deep prayer? and, Is there a way to eliminate a bothersome mental state of fear?

That visit to the retreat-giving hermit, Father William McNamara, was no accident. I know now that God Himself arranged that meeting. I could tell from what happened during the session and afterwards.

I shared with Father Bill all of my fears and feelings.

"Father Sid, you're deep into this friendship already, and let me tell you what the odds are. Very few celibates can have a friendship such as this and remain as single friends, many will leave and marry. Others will break the friendship. That's all I can tell you. Very few can make an 'intimate, celibate, permanent friendship.' " He knew this from all the counseling he did with celibate people, and from his special God-centered wisdom.

Concerning my question on prayer, Father Bill shared one of his ways of prayer and intimacy with the God of all life, love and wisdom:

"First, Father Sid, set a time and place for being alone. Make it a regular time and place preferably. Regardless of circumstances, make time daily or prayer intimacy doesn't grow at its best. We humans need water every day. We need food every day. We need prayer time with God every day. There is no shortcut. Daily bread—daily prayer.

"Second, quiet your mind from all distractions and any cares. Use music or some inspiring literature to help you come to a quiet mind centered on the essentials: life and love. These are simply other names for our great Lord."

The experienced prayerful priest then added, "Most importantly, go to the Word of God after you are quiet and eager to listen to God Himself. Spend time in it and see what your heavenly Father will tell you. He will somehow through His Word talk to you."

This statement would be the beginning of the most significant change in my life. I had always wanted to be a man who could go to God through prayer and then be led by God in every daily event—from the prayer union experience. I had never given God the quiet time or the opportunity to be actively involved in my daily living and loving. I was, by nature and circumstances, more involved in doing God's work as I planned it. I didn't bother going alone to God daily and quietly listening to Him in His directing, empowering Word. That never entered my priestly mind in my eighteen years of honest labor as a priest. I was a sincere work-a-holic for God's church instead of a listening man of prayer who alone can be an authentic man of God. In a way I was a man of God, like a dedicated employee who labors wholeheartedly for a respected company or corporation president.

I realized I was not truly a man of God, a man with an intimate relationship and friendship with His Creator. I knew much about Him from all my training and advanced study. I even met Him a number of times every year in the various sacraments and other special spiritual ministries, but I did not know Him as much as I did Audrey, or my brother Ed, or Mary Jane, or any of my other close friends.

I would never be the same after the conference with Father Bill. Thank God for persons like him. God employed that loving hermit to bring me to the missing link in my life. I mark that time at a Menlo Park retreat center as the beginning of the breakthrough in my life that would lead to permanent health and prosperity. It was centered in a living God of powerful love—Who is my rock foundation.

Nothing, no storm or struggle or failure, has ever weakened that rock relationship. It is a healthy, prosperous believer and lover who is writing this love story for a love-hungry world of lovable and capable people with no rock relationship of intimacy and peace.

Almost everyone I meet, anywhere, any time, expresses in some way that something in life is missing. Each feels unsatisfied with life in general, or unfulfilled, even empty, and sometimes worthless. Some of these people seem to have everything the world calls "making it" ... marriage and family ... excellent position with high-bracket salary ... friends and get-togethers ... maybe more than one home under their ownership. Yet, something is missing inside them that makes them anxious, uneasy, or often restless.

I was like that in my inner self for forty-four years. I had two different degrees given me at different times. Even though I was loved and touched and spoiled by friends for all my priestly years, I was still a restless human being. Something vital was missing. Father Bill graciously entered my life like a once-in-a-lifetime visitor and provided a way to end my life of restlessness that had brought so much inner conflict, confusion, and unhealthy behavior.

Before I left my hermit counselor, I mentioned the question of fears.

He smiled, put his hand on my shoulder and said, "Father Sid, as you grow as a man of listening prayer with God, your intimacy with God will become a fire of powerful, passionate, and tender love. That growing love relationship will conquer any fears—no matter how often they attack."

I said, "Thank you, Father. Please pray for

me and my relationship with God. Together, by God's grace, may we become tremendous Christian lovers."

The love story and events between Audrey and me will demonstrate the road Father Bill pointed out.

Audrey Terkmany, 8th grade graduation.

17

Celibate Friendship

That night Audrey and I discussed the wise hermit's comments. We were pleased that he did none of the decision-making for our lives. He only shared the wisdom of his experiences and his prayerful growth in God.

Audrey and I prayed together. Then we both decided to travel the narrow road of intimate, passionate, celibate friendship. We agreed that such an impossible goal was only reachable by the loving power of the Creator, with whom, the Scripture promises, all things are possible.

As our love-filled relationship grew steadily, the harvest of fruitful ministry around us became abundant. Our firm foundation was God and His mighty Word of truth and power. The sharing love from our God-given friendship was meant to bring forth an abundance of successful ministerial endeavors. Two, in particular, demonstrate God's gracious blessings on the works of His loving believers.

Betty Traynor, the brilliant scientist who taught the public school kids with me, joined in a daring venture of mine, along with a few other ministers and laymen. The dedicated

ecumenical group included Episcopalian, Protestant, Evangelical and Catholic members. We
established a Christian covenant to share our
talents and resources to reach out into the
black and white neighborhood that surrounded
us. We centered ourselves in Almighty God
and His liberating Word under the guidance
and influence of the dynamic Holy Spirit of
God.

We met as a core group weekly and the
benefits from our outreach program enriched
lives, and met the practical needs of youth and
adults. We focused our energies on providing
healthy recreation centers for youth and senior
citizens. We adopted a drug-abuse program
that brought freedom from such deadly addic-
tion, and provided the care in which kids could
discover their worth and the touch of love.

God even arranged for a love-filled priest to
be a member of the Board of Directors of the
community organization. In that role, I had
opportunity to speak in public hearing to the
San Francisco Board of Supervisors. In that
urgent matter, my ecumenical group and
others, especially Betty Traynor and a former
priest, Mike Mooney, turned the public
momentum to our proposal, and thence to
victory. Consequently, Mayor Joseph Alioto
came to our neighborhood for the dedication of
the new facilities.

The other wave of loving outreach I threw
myself into was "little parishes," which was
my most-loved ministry in San Jose. Women
like Flora Raggio, Maureen Weir, Sister
Elizabeth and Father Clem helped me formu-

late and initiate the formation of neighborhood groups of caring believers.

St. Mark's parish was a very multi-cultural assembly. Mostly Negro and Anglo-Catholics, with some Filipinos and some other races. We arranged for black mothers who worked at home to contact the large number of elderly senior Anglo parishioners. The young mothers did the shopping for the shut-in seniors, took them for outings, and cared for them.

The harvest of unity and love was another victory for God's great love power that sees no color or race, only human needs and loving responses. Some of those black mothers were such dynamic people and leaders. I had never worked side by side with my black brothers and sisters before.

One Sunday morning the black priest who regularly celebrated the Mass, culturally adapted to the worship expression of the Afro-Americans, was unexpectedly unable to minister the Mass. I was told that one woman leader told the assembly, "Father Sid is black enough. Will someone go ask him to help us out?"

I accepted and celebrated with all the love that the Holy Spirit poured through me at that unique cultural expression. After Mass my black brothers and sisters hugged and embraced me the way I enjoy doing it—with a lot of soul, and, consequently, with a lot of body.

As the God-centered love flowed between Audrey and me, and then out from us to our parishioners, we found ourselves even more united, more intimate, more outreaching.

With love, Audrey helped my brother Ed and me with our aging Mom and Dad. Mom was now in a well-managed, even caring, convalescent hospital. She had a heart failure condition. However, in her eight years plus in that hospital, she got better and better until her final year of life on earth. Dad, Ed, Audrey and I regularly visited her with a little picnic of goodies. We would sing, touch a lot, and pray together. Mom liked Audrey immediately. I don't know how much Mom realized about the deep friendship between Audrey and me.

In Dad's case, at age 88, he alertly knew my giant affection for Audrey, and he too loved and sang about it. Audrey, with her amazingly striking beauty and loving eyes, brought out the best in my very affectionate Dad.

This growing love relationship of Audrey and me included arguments and temporary separation. Nevertheless our intimacy grew spiritually and physically. We prayed always. We met each other almost every day and embraced more lovingly as time passed. I continued to take her everywhere—to the ecumenical gatherings, to the little parishes, to the community outreach meetings. I was proud of Audrey and of our daring public relationship. Most people accepted and respected our honest, open friendship. A few could not accept our public relationship. Complaining reports were made to church officials.

One day in June, Father Clem called me in for a personal conference—friend to friend.

"Sid, I don't think it is advisable for you to stay here at St. Mark's any longer. Too much pressure all around. I'd appreciate it if you would arrange a transfer by September 15. I'll help you get a good assignment with my high recommendation."

The lightning of Father Clem's recommendation struck with paralyzing force. I excused myself from the conference. My mind was reeling with confusion and fears. I phoned Audrey and arranged to meet her at our special lakeside park. We talked and struggled with a number of major questions: What parish shall I apply for? (At this juncture in clerical history, priests had some say as to where they would minister.) Question number two: What will this change mean to our relationship? (We saw or talked to each other daily and at length.) Question number three: Did our public friendship cause this (terrible to us) turn of events?

Then, more deeply, we faced the harder questions: Shall we continue our deep friendship? (Our public relationship was beginning to rock the established Catholic boat. Maybe we should go underground and into a secret friendship. How about that?)

We held hands as we talked for several hours. We were angry and upset. We felt we had been under unjust attack. We had been public friends on purpose, so that no one would whisper or gossip about some secret unhealthy relationship. We were naive and innocent, and therefore indiscreet. Now the walls of public criticism were tumbling upon us.

After the hours of struggle, we went to our Source, prayer union with the God who had given us to each other for the better times and for the worse times. This was the worst of times.

For a few days we did much soul-searching and deep immersion in God's presence and Word. Sometimes together—more often alone. We reached the agreed decision that it would be healthy and beneficial for us to separate, beginning September 15. It would be a separation for a year to test God's call on us to be intimate friends. Maybe we had fooled ourselves in our deep human need. Maybe ours was a man-made friendship and a destructive one. The personal storm we were in had made things around us and inside of us very unclear and unsettled. We had lost confidence that our love was from God.

It was summer time and Audrey was finishing her Master's Degree in San Francisco. We saw no harm in seeing each other, much less frequently though, until I would be leaving for a new assignment on September 15.

I went to God daily for answers concerning the future of my personal ministry. Soon a practical dream caught my spirit: I would go to the Archbishop with a proposal to open a prayer center in each of the four diocesan counties. I would plan to offer guidance to priests and sisters in the experience of prayer-union with God—both individual and group. Experiences of prayer would be offered and practiced—based on the foundation in the "hermit's" approach, along with some practical innovations of mine. By my sharing with the priests and sisters, they in turn could open prayer centers in their parishes. I envisioned it with a multitude of praying parishioners in prayer union with God Himself, mainly listening to Him. These centers could become places of love, forgiveness, healing and outreach. This would be a miracle from God to us all.

Many believers have too much hurt, resentment and unforgiveness in them to be vessels of love and peace. I was that way until I let God in to do His reconstruction work. Prayer union with a living, speaking God in His powerful Word can do this. My dream was to share God's power through the prayer-center dream.

Audrey loved my dream and encouraged me strongly.

We kept meeting, sharing and embracing, knowing September 15 would be a tough, but needed, experiment. We didn't mention that date often. We simply enjoyed what God was giving us along the way—nourishing friendship, a Master's Degree and my dream of dynamic prayer centers.

In the middle of the summer the Archbishop summoned me to his office. "Father Sid, I think highly of your plan for prayer centers. They are greatly needed to nourish our Catholic people spiritually. However, I can't spare you at this time for that full-time work. I'd appreciate you selecting a parish assignment. I'll tell the pastor to allow you one day a week for your prayer ministry with priests and sisters."

"Thank you, Bishop, for considering this plan of mine that is so important to me. I'm going through some important decision-making at present." Something inside me urged me to tell him more, but I didn't. At the time, I couldn't. Instead, I said, "Bishop, let me check with some parishes and pastors. I'll get back to you by August 15. Is that all right with you?

"Fine, Father Sid. You have a positive record of giving totally wherever you are, even after your sickness. We are very proud of your work."

I left his office with a more unsettled sense of the future. I picked up Audrey and we drove to the beach. We walked for a long time. Then I said, "Want to know what I really want to do? I'd like to take a leave of absence for a year. Many priests have been doing it to settle their doubts and confusions. Some return to ministry, others leave. Most of them go on to marriage."

I could tell Audrey was surprised at my statements. Not shaken, but caught off balance.

"We'd better pray over it, Sid. This is too big a step without the wisdom and support of God."

We prayed. We prayed for two weeks as often as we could. Mostly we prayed alone, but kept in daily touch by phone. On August 15, we drove to the beach again.

"What I'm going to do, Audrey, is tell the Bishop that I want to be assigned to St. Anthony's in Menlo Park. My best priest friend is pastor, Father Johnny Coleman. He's a real prince. That way I'll be away from the city and you for a while. I'll tell Johnny that I'm thinking over my priesthood life. He'll understand and accept me. How does that sound to you?"

"I wish you weren't going that far away." (It was only 30 miles.) "But we agreed to separate in order to let God tell us what He wants for us. Tell the Bishop, Sid. If he's wise, he'll gladly send you to a happy rectory and a highly-respected pastor."

Things happened so quickly after that. The Bishop approved the transfer. I packed my belongings for the tenth time in my nineteen years as a priest and headed for a crucial year of labor and decision.

Father Johnny accepted me with open arms and an open mind. He had always had me in his heart of friendship. Often he'd say publicly: "This is Father Sid, the only man I know that the 400 priests of the diocese love." It was an exaggeration, of course, yet it always felt so good to hear it.

I told him about my year to think things over and possibly leave parish-priest ministry. He understood and said he would be with me whatever my final choice.

Immediately, I threw myself into the three special works I volunteered to do. Johnny approved and gave the needed assistance. His was a large congregation of Anglo-Catholics and Hispanic Catholics—Hispanic majority of three to one, perhaps. I would be ministering among them, to the Kaiser Hospital patients, to the teenagers, and to adults desiring Vatican II renewal.

The first month there the work was very fulfilling. I worked with enthusiasm, but in quiet moments I missed Audrey immensely. Our phone calls were daily and love-filled. Our separation obviously wasn't a total one. My phone bill that month was $119 . . . nearly half of my month's salary. No wonder I had to have my own phone!

Audrey and I kept praying. God kept in touch with us in His Word. We relied totally on His Word. A good shepherd, like God, would lead us wisely. We had come to believe that in the deepest part of our being. We had no guru but God. We were risking our entire lives on Him and His guiding Word. Risking oneself on God, I know now, is the surest way to wisdom and strength. True, we were new in God's personal intimacy, we were anxious, but we trusted Him nevertheless.

God broke through the confusion in our lives. He blesses anyone who trusts totally in Him. We had in some degree of consciousness surrendered our lives and future into His hands. God spoke clearly: first to Audrey, then to me.

After I met Audrey in our favorite park, she said firmly but haltingly, "Sid, I realize now that I can no longer grow as God wants me to if I stay in my religious community. I've prepared a letter of resignation. I want you to read it and give me your comments."

I read the letter carefully, and was filled with an inner peace that only a God of love can give. She was honestly leaving her community at God's invitation, and not on account of me. I was ecstatic because she was willing to follow

God and His loving Word under any human pressures.

Two months later we walked down the front stairs of her community residence. At the curb outside her convent was parked a new green automobile. Enterprisingly, I had borrowed $100 from each of ten priests. I told them I needed the money to help a friend in an urgent emergency. The bank approved the loan and down payment as long as I would co-sign the papers. Audrey had no established credit rating in the secular world. I told her proudly, and with a Filipino twinkle, "You have me, honey, and a lot of clerical backers!"

I had promised to pay the priests back within 30 days. I went back to the same bank that gave clerics preferential service. No priest till that time had failed on any loan commitment. I took out a second loan with my car as collateral and paid the ten clergy investors their money back within two weeks. Crazy wisdom, indeed, but necessities of love can beget such inventions.

With pride and enthusiasm I drove Audrey in her new economy car to moderately-priced apartments in the Redwood City area, adjacent to Menlo Park. She chose a third-floor, one-bedroom apartment. We know the Lord arranged this. A young teacher was moving out in two days to go to an Oregon position. He needed transportation money immediately. Audrey, who had only $800 (her community departure gift), offered him $175 for his furniture. He had wanted $200, but was desperate and took her offer, and said he would leave the next day. As we left in a triumphal mood, I managed to slip him another $25.

The following day I took Audrey to a job interview that I had arranged through a special contact, a former priest now in the insurance business. She did well in the screening and interview, was hired and told to report to the San Jose job on the Monday after Christmas. This meant she had a five-day vacation to set up her apartment and get ready for her new adventure as assistant coordinator of a Catholic organization which helped the hungry and homeless.

Audrey (Postulant) 1954, and her mother, Marion Terkmany.

18

Leaving the System

When Audrey began her new work, I also jumped into an ocean of tasks at St. Anthony's. These were to be my final six months as a parish priest. Thanks to God, they were the most joyous. However, immense gratitude for my happy spirit and ministry was owed to Father Johnny Coleman, my pastor and friend of thirty years.

Johnny is a mixture of the poverty of Francis of Assisi and the dedicated work of Theresa of Calcutta. He owns nothing for any period of time. Everything he receives he gives to someone who needs it. One Christmas his family gave him a special guitar, with a contract that forbade the transfer of the instrument to anyone. He signed the contract and kept it for three years—until he met an alcoholic who needed it to help him survive. The sick person survived and put the guitar in a pawn shop ... then Johnny bought the guitar back from the pawnbroker. Johnny ministered endlessly and in many directions—sometimes all at once. He worked until he collapsed into a chair at midnight.

He had the gifts of humor, music and

encouragement. Because he spoke Spanish he developed a multi-cultured Christian community. The people worked together and opened a dining room for the needy and lonely. Daily three hundred persons benefited from the generous nourishment. Johnny also made available all the unused, unpaved grounds for vegetable planting. Everyone was welcome to plant, harvest and share with others.

Johnny stood by me as a loyal friend that whole year, encouraging and congratulating my ministry endeavors. He met and liked Audrey. He was glad she helped me with my work with the teenagers and the adults. She felt accepted and comfortable at St. Anthony's parish.

A highlight of St. Anthony's was the thirty-minute prayer sessions (which later turned into two-hour sessions). We began with five brother priests: Fathers Frank, Don, Sandy, Bob, Skip and me. These prayer meetings were again based on the hermit's recommendations: music, Scripture, quiet time and optional sharing. The prayer nourishment developed our spiritual lives and made our ministries more effective. In the dinners after the meetings, we sang, told funny incidents, shared the latest news around the diocese, and relaxed.

Changes were coming about in the Catholic Church in many ways. In one parish 900 parishioners met to vote unanimously to keep their much-loved, dedicated pastor who had gotten married. This was a victory of sorts. However, the Bishop voted negative to the issues and Father Bob (my Pacifica pastor) was released of his duties. He went into community counseling service.

The priest brothers supported me during my year of decision. I didn't tell Audrey for I wished to check myself out completely before my departure into the new lifestyle outside the parish priesthood.

First, I went to a well-recommended internist for a battery of tests from head to toe. "All clear" was the strong verdict. Victory number one: a physical victory.

Next, I chose a psychiatrist of local renown. I began career and transition counseling. After all, I was taking a big step in leaving an environment that was mine since age fifteen. We discussed much the fact that someday I might marry. After a number of sessions I said, "Dr. Martin, I'm ready."

"Father Sid, you were ready three weeks ago!"

Victory number two. I did all of these examinations because of my total burnout fifteen years earlier. Now I was ready for another victory, the big victory.

Audrey drove down the scenic coastline and parked near the ocean which delighted us so much. We walked for a while then sat on some large chunks of wood.

"Audrey, I've decided for sure. I'll be leaving in June, on my twentieth anniversary. I've been checking out some job opportunities. I want to start work by July." I easily detected her facial expression of calm joy and happy eyes. I continued a bit more slowly:

"I've prayed extra long about something and all I get is the big green light from God. I want to marry you. I want you to consider the matter at length before you answer. I'm being honest with you, as always, I am not leaving the parish priesthood to marry you. After twenty years of ministry, I cannot be healthy —physically, emotionally or even spiritually—without a daily companion. I need one to love, touch and encourage me, and to root for me, no matter what. I'd rather be single and celibate yet have such an intimate companion as you have been. But the church system is not in favor of that kind of relationship. God wants me healthy. I can't love and serve others while destroying myself. God says to love others as we love ourselves. Audrey, I'm going with God, and leaving the system. I want to make it in the work world, and when I do I'd like to marry you."

I don't remember how loud the ocean waves were that day. I heard Audrey very clearly, "When you're free to marry and ready, I'll gladly marry you. The thought has crossed my mind, you know, for I felt you would be leaving something that has kept you from working healthily and happily."

This was the most breath-taking experience in my God-protected journey—offering marriage and having the offer accepted! So many people must have prayed for me all my life—parents, family, grammar school nuns, all the parishioners, the Cursillo and university friends, and all the other people who loved me for my personal, spiritual ministry. Those prayers of faith moved the mountains in my fear-filled, love-hungry life. A loving God, who answers all faith prayers, sent to me the precious blessing of the perfect woman. Without God and Audrey I would be like a splendid jet airplane with one wing, no engines, and no navigator.

Through people's prayers, and my own gradual walk through prayer, I received from God the unique life partner I needed. Audrey is to me like the other wing if I were to fly always as a capable, loving person. God, at my daily invitation, furnishes all the engine power and fuel. He has also shared His special Helper the Holy Spirit, as my navigating guide.

At God's calling, I was leaving the parish ministry to follow His directions and plan. I knew I would follow Him wherever and always because of the total personal commitment in my spirit to the living God of love that I finally met at the age of forty-four. It was a forever commitment. I'm only human, and forever is a tough word to live up to—God makes the difference. My commitment to Him is forever—thanks to His powerful grace.

The last two months at St. Anthony's were only a joyous blurr. On my twentieth anniversary I had my farewell to one lifestyle, and the beginning of a new Christian journey. I was to offer the Mass, but the Bishop whom I had visited in April to take care of the necessary steps in leaving called and said to have another priest celebrate the Mass. Because of the peacefulness in me, I said quietly, "I didn't mean anything public or disturbing, Bishop.

I'll have Father Coleman offer the Mass."

A former priest commented at the celebration: "Sid, this is a first in history, a priest leaving in a celebration of Mass dedicated to his service and to his new direction on the outside."

I didn't know it was a first. I certainly knew that God encouraged a multitude of people to love me during the twenty-year journey. God knew how love hungry I was. Dominic, one of the Christian leaders of the parish, provided a luncheon fit for royalty. I loved all my loyal and royal friends.

Two days later I left St. Anthony's parish with Father Johnny Coleman's special blessing, embrace, and a special wallet with $100 in it. As I drove away I was singing one of my favorite songs, "Born Free." I knew deep down that I was no longer a love-hungry priest. I was a love-filled man.

19

The Post-Priesthood Years

Eight years ago I left St. Anthony's as a love-filled man. Those eight years have been struggles, failures and victories. Such is the ordinary journey of a love-filled believer. Thanks to the God of power and intimacy, I am today a more abundantly love-filled and love-overflowing person. God is love and an intimate relationship with Him has poured dynamic, life-changing love through my entire being, and then outward into my family, friends, and the world around me. I had dared to experience genuine and strong love that withstood the pressures and distractions of a demanding world.

The first major struggle after my parish departure was finding a job. I searched and interviewed without success. For four months straight Father Johnny Coleman visted my brother Ed and me in my apartment the first of the month, and while hugging me put $100 in my pocket. Then I got a break.

A public school teacher needed an immediate operation and recommended me as the one to handle her difficult group of students. I have taught since that day. One year while teaching my body sounded the alarm of sweating and chills due to heavy stress. I quit the job, but God made a victory from an apparent failure. It seemed I was being led in circles before I reached my "land of promise" employment: Woodside Public High School. I've been teaching the Latin language there for four years now. Classes have grown from twenty to over seventy students. This professional position is an educational, God-given blessing to me. I respect and teach the lovable and capable students as though they were my own sons and daughters.

In Audrey's case, employment has been a year-to-year challenge or crisis. Neither of us knows from year to year if we have jobs. She is now a tenured teacher, however, low in seniority. I am still on temporary contract. God has made a way where there is no apparent way.

Audrey's and my wondrous intimacy blossomed into marriage on August 2, 1975. A number of friends urged us to a much earlier date. We knew, however, we had to establish a reasonable stability in finances, and also to give our relationship more time to ripen in the bigger world.

The hundred guests enjoyed the entire wedding and festivities. The music themes of the wedding were an instrumental recording of "Camelot" as Audrey proceeded into our midst. "You've Got a Friend" was the other major theme in song. A beloved priest, Father Jim, witnessed the marriage ceremony. Audrey and I exchanged the marriage vows (of our own creation) and promised each other a forever friendship, by God's grace and calling. The rings were shaped as small, regal crowns—always to remind us of that Christian ceremony, and more deeply of our belonging to the family of the King of kings. Some friends arranged the memorable outdoor reception as a wedding gift.

We spent two days of our honeymoon at the nearby Royal Coach Hotel. As part of our honeymoon we flew to New Jersey to celebrate with Audrey's family.

During the difficult days of unemployment in our lives, our married intimacy and sharing communication were strained. We found ourselves quarreling and arguing more frequently. But we had pledged ourselves to sharing openly any hurts, resentments, or misunderstandings. At times, the marriage storms were raging tempests, but we hung to our commitment. Somehow by nighttime we managed to be somewhat settled. We were not at peace, however, as individuals or in our companionship. We didn't fully realize why the marriage problems were growing rather than diminishing. In 1978 God established a breakthrough for us.

A family in our neighborhood, Bob and Diane Jasey, mentioned the Catholic Marriage Encounter Retreat. "You two would love it," bubbled Diane in genuine enthusiasm.

"It's a great experience for couples who want a weekend together," smiled witty Bob.

"Do you have to share publicly with other couples?" Audrey inquired.

"Not at all," Bob quickly asserted.

Audrey and I signed the necessary papers for the retreat.

That marriage encounter weekend brought remarkable blessings to our relationship. Disillusionments are part of the marriage journey. Dealing with them and building again is what most married couples omit. Disenchantment is only a siren calling them to check for causes and build again the fire of love.

Audrey and I realized the major weakness in our married life. During the pressures of our unsettled employment status we turned insecure and anxious. Instead of going to intimacy with God in His encouraging Word, we turned inward and to silence. We repressed the pent-up feelings of insecurity and the growing sense of inadequacy. The consequences were a shaky relationship and a marriage growing dull.

On the Sunday morning dialogue between Audrey and me—a three-hour session—we told each other our discoveries of the weekend. We emptied the emotional garbage. We shared renewed goals and practical daily steps to a great married love. In the midst of that session, Audrey and I were locked in each other's embrace as we laughed and cried, and even did both at the same time. In our spirits we were locked fast again, with God in the midst of the bond.

An occasion calling for overflowing love was the Silver Anniversary of my class. The married classmates were invited to participate at a banquet. Before I went, I spent some time in prayer that afternoon in the major seminary, which is only a few blocks from my home. In the quiet of that chapel, where I had worshipped for six years long ago, I knelt and made a gift to the great God of love with Whom I was now intimate. In those earlier years, I had mostly known Him in a mental relationship. On this occasion I listened to Him and offered Him the supreme gift.

I prayed, "Father, Source of all love, You are first in my life, You and You alone. You are my source, my fire, my purpose. You have allowed me to enjoy an intimate union with You for some years now. You have given me Audrey as my wife and great love. I now offer You, in my new health and new life of love, my whole being in total surrender. Total surrender into Your wise plans. When I quarterbacked my life's plans I suffered defeat—and after the defeat even a total burnout. I hand my life and future entirely into Your care. I totally trust You. I will always listen to Your directions. Here I am, Father."

That total surrender is difficult for most human beings. Yet, that step of total gift of self (and self-centeredness) opens the floodgates of God's abounding love, peace and joy. This total gift of one's self begins the process of a person progressing toward total realization of all one's positive desires and dreams.

That prayer session made it an easy journey to San Francisco for the Silver Anniversary get-together. I was the only married former classmate in attendance. Of the twenty classmates, eight left the ministry, two died, and ten are still active.

Since my total surrender to God, each day is an adventure. This adventure includes struggles and victories, even failures often before eventual victories. Life with God is never a dull relationship. He is a loving God of surprises and strength. He answers all needs and dreams. The timetable, however, belongs to Him. From my experience of the last nine years, God is never too early in answering me, nevertheless, He is never late.

At a Charismatic Prayer Group, I decided to go through the experience of inviting the Holy Spirit into my life. I was already totally surrendered to God. The final step was to allow myself, like willing clay in the hands of a powerful potter, to invite the Holy Spirit with all of His various gifts, into my deepest being.

The Holy Spirit's work is to lead us to the fullest realization of God's total purpose in our life. The Holy Spirit helps us reach our highest dreams, even the impossible ones. I prayed and received. The Holy Spirit came and filled me, as Jesus promised.

From then on I knew it wasn't what I did or could do. It was what Jesus Christ had done that would give me life, life everlasting. The Holy Spirit's fire and gifts would make overflowing love pour in and through my heart, and into the world around me.

The spiritual experience was a gentle, yet powerful one—like wind. As love-filled believers, now led from within by the Holy Spirit of God, brother Ed, Audrey and I live in

the real world of struggles and pressures with a
deep inner peace, joy and power. We are ready
and eager for each day's challenges and opportunities.

Yes, I am ready for any call of God on my
life, more so now than twenty-eight years ago
on my ordination day. As a love-filled believer I
make quiet time each day, and I listen to the
Spirit of God in the Scriptural Word of life. I
am ready for any event as long as I hear in the
Word the invitation: "Come, follow me, Sid, for
My love and strength will always be with you."

Some of the personal communications and
encouragement that God shares with me on my
daily journey are:

> "Be concerned above everything else
> with the Kingdom of God and with
> what he requires of you, and he will
> provide you with all these other
> things" (Matt. 6:33, TEV).

> "And it is he who will supply all your
> needs from his riches in glory,
> because of what Christ Jesus has
> done for us" (Phil. 4:19, LB).

> "I can do everything God asks me to
> do with the help of Christ who gives
> me the strength and power" (Phil.
> 4:13, LB).

> "For the Spirit that God has given us
> does not make us timid; instead, his

Spirit fills us with power, love, and self-control" (2 Tim. 1:7, TEV).

"Seek your happiness in the Lord, and he will give you your heart's desire. Give yourself to the Lord; trust in him, and he will help you; he will make your righteousness shine like the noonday sun" (Ps. 37:4-5, TEV).

"The Lord is my shepherd; I have everything I need. He lets me rest in fields of green grass and leads me to quiet pools of fresh water. He gives me new strength" (Ps. 23:1-3, TEV).

"You didn't choose me! I chose you! I appointed you to go and produce lovely fruit always, so that no matter what you ask for from the Father, using my name, he will give it to you" (John 15:16, LB).

"And I am sure that God who began the good work within you will keep right on helping you grow in his grace until his task within you is finally finished on that day when Jesus Christ returns" (Phil. 1:6, LB).

My life at last is one of simplicity and balance, spirituality and abundance, struggles and victories. How can this be? My life is rooted in a living God of love and power—and in my God-given wife, Audrey. With a love-filled heart, I praise and thank God for letting me know that it was not good for THIS MAN to be alone.

My love-filled Christian journey continues . . .

HOW TO EXPERIENCE THE
BAPTISM IN THE HOLY SPIRIT

"Something is happening in America, some new sign of hope, some star in the darkness: you are not only rediscovering Jesus as Lord, you are also rediscovering that the Spirit of Jesus is alive today and working in your midst. The accentuation of the Holy Spirit in our times is certainly a sign of hope, but we need more than right thinking about the Holy Spirit: we need a renewed encounter with, a new surrender to, the Holy Spirit. I seriously believe that in this Charismatic renewal there is something very important for the renewal of the Church, something that will help us toward a real, visible unity with God. I think that we have here one of the wonders of God today." —Cardinal Leo Josef Suenens

First of all, never forget that Jesus is the Baptizer. Don't seek an experience, but seek Jesus Christ and His Kingdom. This is a gift of God, not a sacrament nor a substitute for a sacrament. It can be a dynamic response to and release of all you have known in Baptism and Confirmation. You cannot earn it, nor do you deserve it, but you should follow certain guidelines to experience it according to the Scripture given in John 1:33: "But I did not recognize him. The one who sent me to baptize with water told me, 'When you see the Spirit descend and rest on someone, it is he who is to baptize with the Holy Spirit.' Now I have seen for myself and have testified, 'This is God's chosen One.'"

HAVE YOU A PERSONAL
RELATIONSHIP WITH JESUS?

To experience the baptism you need first to make sure that you have accepted Jesus as your personal Savior and have been born again. The baptism in the Holy Spirit is only given to the believer. It is a separate experience from water baptism. "John baptized with water, but within a few days you will be baptized with the Holy Spirit" (Acts 1:15). In the first we experience a **PRESENCE**—in the second a full release of **POWER** as we are immersed in God's Spirit.

BE SURE THERE IS NO UNCONFESSED
SIN IN YOUR LIFE

If there is someone whom you have not forgiven, or if you are aware of bitterness, hatred or resentment in your heart, make your peace with God and man.

TAKE AUTHORITY OVER DEMONIC
CONTROL

In the past if you have gone to the fortune teller, used horoscopes, Ouija board, mind control, ESP, hypnotism, yoga, automatic writing, or even if you have read books by clairvoyants, renounce these in the name of Jesus.

ASK JESUS TO FULLY RELEASE WITHIN
YOU THE POWER OF HIS HOLY SPIRIT—
TO BAPTIZE YOU IN THE HOLY SPIRIT

Put away all fears. "For God has not given us the spirit of fear, but of power, love and a sound mind" (1 Timothy 1:7). Sometimes it is more effective to have a group of Spirit-baptized

Christians pray with you. However, if you don't know of such a group, don't let this hinder you from praying the following prayer.

Dear Jesus, Your Word says in Revelation 3:20, "Behold I stand at the door and knock, if anyone hears my voice and opens the door I will come in . . ." Jesus, I open the door of my heart. Come in and be my personal Savior. Thank You for keeping Your Word.

Jesus, I am sorry for all the times that I have sinned. Forgive me, take away all my bitterness, my hatred and my resentment. I forgive _____ (Name those you need to forgive) even as you have forgiven me.

I renounce Satan and all his work and all the kingdoms of darkness. I renounce any power in me that is not under the lordship of Jesus Christ. I renounce despair, discouragement and seeing myself as worthless. I take You Jesus as my Lord and Savior, my deliverer from all evil, and my healer from all sickness and the scars of my past life.

I accept myself as mightily loved by God the Father. I accept myself as powerfully saved by God the Son. I accept the Holy Spirit as promised of the Father, as my Counselor, my Comforter, my Teacher, and my pledge of the Kingdom of love forever.

Jesus, baptize me now in Your Holy Spirit. Fully release within me all the power, all the gifts, and all the fruit of Your Holy Spirit. Release within me a new power to praise You both in English and tongues. As a response of faith I will now praise You in my new prayer language. In Jesus' name, Amen.

AFTER THE BAPTISM OF THE HOLY SPIRIT

The purpose of this new relationship with God: His Spirit is forming Christ's life in you so that you may accomplish the Father's will. "And you also became God's people when you heard the true message, the Good News that brought you salvation. You believed in Christ, and God put his stamp of ownership on you by giving you the Holy Spirit he had promised. The Spirit is the guarantee that we shall receive what God has promised his people, and this assures us that God will give complete freedom to those who are his. Let us praise his glory!" (Eph. 1:13-14, TEV).

Rejoice in the Trinity: the companionship of the Holy Spirit, union with Jesus, the loving care of our Father. One should never feel alone after receiving the baptism in the Holy Spirit. Know that God enjoys your companionship and wants you to enjoy His. "He carries out and fulfills all of God's promises, no matter how many of them there are; and we have told everyone how faithful he is, giving glory to his name. It is this God who has made you and me into faithful Christians and commissioned us apostles to preach the Good News. He has put his brand upon us—his mark of ownership—and given us his Holy Spirit in our hearts as guarantee that we belong to him, and as the first installment of all that he is going to give us" (1 Cor. 1:20-22, TLB).

Don't worry about:

• what to do; the Holy Spirit's **wisdom** is available to you (1 Cor. 2:6-13);

• how to do it; the Holy Spirit's **power** is available to you (Luke 23:49);

• what to say; the Holy Spirit will **teach** you (Luke 12:11-12);

• what you are; be patient with your faults and

failings. Cooperate patiently with the Holy Spirit's work of sanctification in you (2 Pet. 1:3-11).

Rededicate yourself to your vocation in life; re-examine your responsibilities, your relationships to your family, church, community, co-workers. Express your love of God in service of others (Matt. 25:31-46).

Keep yourself free to recognize and respond to the promptings of the Holy Spirit. This means casting out fear and inhibition (2 Tim. 1:7). Pray for discernment of spirits. Seek guidance when it is available.

Be ready to witness to the Good News when the occasion is offered. Speak of God's goodness to you (John 9:1-38) and the reason why you believe in His promise.

Learn to pray always, thanking God for His goodness to you and simply and joyfully praising that infinite goodness. Pray for your needs, those of the community, the Church, all mankind. You have an efficacious power in prayer now; you have only to use it confidently. "Praying always with all prayer and supplication in the Spirit, and watching thereunto with all perseverance and supplication for all saints" (Eph. 6:18). Adapt your prayer to your attractions and circumstances. The Psalms will help you to praise God. Keep your prayer life simple and spontaneous. Spend some time alone with God each day. Christ often went aside to pray alone (Matt. 14:23; Luke 6:12).

Read Scripture often (2 Tim. 3:14-17; 2 Pet. 1:16-21). This will strengthen your faith that God has fulfilled His promise to send you the Holy Spirit in all His POWER. Read books that will nourish your prayer life and lead you to a deeper knowledge of the wonderful works of God, especially through Jesus.

Be faithful to your chosen prayer group. Christ makes Himself known most clearly through the Holy Spirit's action within a body of believers. Be assured that you will grow in the life of the Holy Spirit within the community of believers in which you embarked upon a life of faith and confidence in the power of the Holy Spirit. "I am in the midst of you" (Romans 8:14-30).